SCOTSTYLE
150 YEARS OF
SCOTTISH
ARCHITECTURE

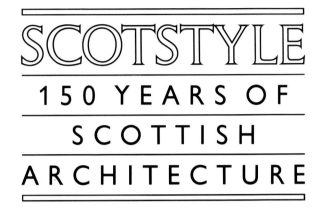

SCOTSTYLE
150 YEARS OF
SCOTTISH
ARCHITECTURE

by Fiona Sinclair
with an Introduction by Colin McWilliam
Concluding Essay by David J Leslie

Published by
The Royal Incorporation of Architects in Scotland
and the Scottish Academic Press
ISBN 0 7073 0418 0 (Casebound)
ISBN 0 7073 0422 9 (Paperbound)

Published by The Royal Incorporation of
Architects in Scotland, 15 Rutland Square,
Edinburgh and the Scottish Academic Press,
33, Montgomery Street, Edinburgh
First published 1984

British Library Cataloguing in Publication Data

Sinclair, Fiona
    Scotstyle.
    1. Architecture, Modern—19th century—
    Scotland   2. Architecture, Modern—20th
    century—Scotland   3. Architecture—
    Scotland
    I. Title
    720′.9411   NA978

ISBN 0 7073 0418 0 (Casebound)
ISBN 0 7073 0422 9 (Paperbound)

Designed by Forth Studios Ltd, Edinburgh
Printed in Great Britain by
Clark Constable
Edinburgh   London   Melbourne

Acknowledgements

A study of the breadth and nature of *Scotstyle* must necessarily lean heavily on the writings and research of others. The Working Group of David J Leslie, Anne Millin, David Page, Fiona Sinclair and, in particular, Michael Vipond, whose task it was to obtain the information and photographs used in the preparation of both publication and exhibition, are indebted to the following for their assistance:

David Walker, who provided numerous notes and pointers of reference, and who read and corrected the text. Dr Frank Walker, who did likewise, and John Hume and Frank Worsdall who were able to provide invaluable items of information. David S Cameron, John Duncan, Alan Harrison, John Lane, Ian McGill, Harry McNab, Peter Robinson, Colin Wishart and Andrew Wright, all of the RIAS and all of whom were able to provide information on various buildings in the selection. Charles McKean, who lent stimulus and advice; Kit Campbell whose original idea it was in 1981; Colin McWilliam who kindly wrote an introduction and provided notes, and John Richards who chaired the Selection Committee. The Universities of Aberdeen, Glasgow and Strathclyde assisted in the gathering of information, as did the staff of the Mitchell Library, Glasgow, the staff of the Royal Commission on Ancient and Historic Monuments in Scotland, and members of Glasgow District Council's Planning Department, the Highland District Council's Planning Department, Perth and Kinross District Council's Planning Department, Strathclyde Regional Council and Tayside Regional Council's Architects' Department. The following kindly supplied notes and theses on individual buildings — Neil Baxter, Janet R Blair, Cheah, James Craven, Ramsay Gray, D S Haggart, Lesley Kerr, David Laing, Lady Iona Mackworth-Young, Sonya McAngus, David McIntosh, John McManus and Lawrence McCluskey, Ray O'Donnell, Charles Redmond, John Soutar and Ian Trotter. Assistance was also given by Barclay Curle and Company, William Dick, John Gifford, David Hayes of Landmark, A Hunter of Mount Stuart, Dr James MacAuley, Dr Ronald MacFadzean, Irene McGeoch, Malcolm Mitchell, National Coal Board (Scottish Division), Major and Mrs Nicolson of 'Cour', Royal Bank of Scotland (Properties Department), Royal College of Physicians' Hall, Edinburgh, Jack Sloan, Lesley Stevenson, Michael Thornley and Peter Willis. In addition, many architects and firms of architects provided information and illustrations of their buildings. Gillian MacKinnon assisted in the preparation of the indices and with the typing.

Scotstyle was made possible through the generous sponsorship of the Miller Group.

Photographic Acknowledgements

The following kindly permitted publication of their photographs:

Aberdeen University Library (1900); Anderson, Kininmonth and Paul, Rowand (1952); T and R Annan (1855 1859); *The Architects' Journal* (1906 1956 1958); *The Architectural Digest* (1903); Boswell Mitchell and Johnston (1973); Brett, Studio (1965); British Tourist Authority (1940); Burnett, Ralph (1897); Charles, Martin (1980); Connolly, Gerry (1979); *Country Life Magazine* (1901); Crumlish, Alan (1863 1873 *exterior* 1889 *detail* 1891 *detail* 1915 1917 1919 1930 1935 1948 1949); Cumbernauld Development Corporation (1961); The Dept. of the Environment (1836 *main picture* 1967); Dick, William (1872 1881 1923 *detail*); Dunbar, David (1873 *interior*); Fenwick, Hubert (1852); Gillanders and Mack Photography (1955); Gillespie, Kidd and Coia (1931 1957 *main picture* 1962); Glasgow District Council Planning Department (1936); Glasgow University Archives (1922 1939); Hamilton, Ian (1977); Hayes, David (1969); The Reverend Henderson (1935); Highland District Council Planning Department (1847); Hume, John R (1857 1886 1905 1908 1918); Alastair Hunter Photography (1950 1968 1975 1983); Hunterian Art Gallery, Glasgow (1904); Innes, Hector (1972); Kersting, Anthony (1844 1845 1851 1861 *detail* 1893 1895); Law and Dunbar-Nasmith (1976 *exterior*); J M Lawson (1938); Lady Iona Mackworth-Young (1876); The Mitchell Library, Glasgow (1853 *exterior* 1858 1860 *perspective* 1869 1877 1891 1892 1899 1920); John Moffat Photographer (1974); Montgomerie, Bryan (1864); Morris and Steedman (1963); P and W MacLellan (1880); McGill, Ian (1911); McKean, Charles (1916 1933); McManus, John and McCluskey, Lawrence (1914); National Coal Board, Scottish Division (1954); The National Galleries of Scotland (1834); The National Trust for Scotland (1902); Newberg, Sidney (1934); Niven, Douglas (1979); Perth and Kinross District Council Planning Department (1838 *gates* 1928); Perth Art Gallery and Museum (1838 *dairy, square* 1870 1878); Ray Prographics (1952); Reiach, John (1910); J Roman Rock (1953 1966); The Royal Commission on Ancient and Historic Monuments in Scotland (1837 1838 *library* 1839 1840 1842 1843 1848 1849 1853 *interior* 1854 1856 1860 *elevation* 1862 1866 1867 1868 1871 1874 1875 1879 1883 1884 1885 1887 1889 1890 1896 1898 1901 *detail* 1912 1924 1925 1927 1932 1937); Sinclair, Fiona (1836 *detail* 1848 *plan* 1861 *main picture*); Henk Snoek Reprints (1964 1970 1971 1976 *interior*); Spanphoto (1913 1978 1981); Swain, Studio (1951); Tayside Regional Council Architects' Department (1907); Vipond, Michael (1846 1894 1923 1926 1929 1959); Dr Frank Walker (1841); Whyler Photographs (1888); Wilson, G Forrest (1957 *detail*); Wilson, Rob (1982); Wishart, Colin (1865 1882 1946 1947); Worsdall, Frank (1850); Wrightson, David (1909); Wylie Shanks and Partners (1960).

McIntosh, David (cover photograph — St. Vincent Chambers, Glasgow)

Preface

Fiona Sinclair

1834 may seem an arbitrary point at which to begin a descriptive account of the development of Scottish architecture, but it coincides with the foundation of the Royal Institute of British Architects, the oldest professional architectural institute in the world whose 150th anniversary in 1984 was marked by the launch of the Festival of Architecture.

Scotstyle represents only one of the many commemorative events staged by the RIBA's sister organisation, the Royal Incorporation of Architects in Scotland. Written to accompany a travelling exhibition of the same name, it is intended to serve as a record of Scotland's architectural progress over the last 150 years, and to stimulate interest in the country's built environment and heritage.

The buildings illustrated were selected from over 750 nominations made by public and practitioners alike. A jury chaired by John Richards — President of the RIAS — and which included David Walker, Dr Frank Walker, Professor Andrew MacMillan, Robert Steedman, Charles McKean, Neil Baxter and Colin McWilliam, selected — for each year since the inauguration of the RIBA — a building (or group of buildings) which was deemed to have made a significant, innovative, interesting or, quite simply, enjoyable contribution to Scotland's architectural fabric of the time. In order to simplify the selection procedure, only buildings which are still extant were considered, with the one exception of Glasgow's Empire Exhibition (1938) which, from the very outset, was of a temporary nature, and whose demolition was only hastened by the Second World War.

Of the buildings selected, some have weathered better than others. The final selection, however, while an undeniably incongruous collection of architectural sizes, shapes and styles, does represent a range of buildings which share a curious, indomitable confidence — from the purposeful Grecian of Edinburgh's Royal Scottish Academy (1834), through to the leisurely *rightness* of the Burrell Gallery in Glasgow (1983).

Is there an identifiable Scottish style in architecture? In all likelihood the answer is "yes", but this selection — "architectural cake rather than . . . bread and butter" — provides us with clues rather than hard evidence. What is important, however, is that the buildings featured in *Scotstyle* have a sense of belonging — a head start if there ever was one.

Introduction

Colin McWilliam (author of *Scottish Townscape* and *Lothian*)

This is a celebration of a hundred and fifty years of architecture which we are proud to possess in 1984, and of its designers.

Scotstyle is about actual buildings — each one in its context answering a set of functional, structural and aesthetic needs, and combining all the answers into a single distinctive answer which is what we call Architecture. It brings together, in the rather arbitrary pattern of one building per year, a story of continuous and still largely unrecognised achievement.

Unrecognised? People's feelings about "buildings" (the ones they know and use) are often oddly different from their feelings about "architecture". The latter is a form of high art which they make special visits to see and admire, and which tends to stop somewhere about 1830. There is so much before that date, finishing with that marvellous hundred-year plateau of systematic elegance — delightfully varied by the picturesque movement — which we call Georgian. After that date, and about the time *Scotstyle* begins, the story changes. Buildings and periods are lumped together into stereotypes like fussy, pretentious Victorian, pompous Edwardian, the jazzy twenties and thirties, itsy-bitsy Festival of Britain and so on. Apart from the blatant silliness of treating Victorian as one period, the trouble is that each period is still judged by the clever and satirical things that were said about it by the people who came immediately afterwards. Things are different in the antique trade, where the power of instant nostalgia makes everything up to the day before yesterday — even the rubbish — instantly desirable.

Scotstyle is a fascinating survey of this no-man's land of taste, in which the work of architect 'A' is seen alongside that of architect 'B' who reacted from his principles so sharply, along with architect 'C', who had no time for either of them. Luckily our job is not to decide which architect, or which of their patrons, was right. It is simply to take stock of what they all gave us, and its value to us today.

You may well find (as I do) some of your favourites left out, but the pattern of distribution over the map of Scotland seems fair, with thirty-seven each from Edinburgh and Glasgow; then Dundee (nine), Aberdeen (four), Inverness and Stirling (three each), Paisley (two) and Perth (one). Outside the big towns Strathclyde (twenty-one) and Tayside (twelve) are well ahead, leaving the other regions in single figures and Dumfries and Galloway nowhere. But remember, these figures are not necessarily an indication of overall quality — or lack of it. There has been a tendency to choose, quite naturally, high-style architectural cake rather than just good bread and butter.

An analysis of building types shows an equally clear pattern, with each type (even the twelve country houses and their dependencies) quite evenly divided between the first and second half of the period. Some types have changed their function and image more than others. For example, the Universities of Glasgow (1874, gothic), Edinburgh (1875, Italian) and Aberdeen (1900, gothic) all went in for monumental composition, an image only quite recently superseded by the functional picturesque of Stirling (1974). Schools started as local monuments like the Blythswood Testimonial at Renfrew (1841), but their image was transformed much sooner, following the Education Act of 1872. The Scottish Board School, represented by Scotland Street School in Glasgow (1904) and Stobswell in Dundee (1907) became a classic type in itself. Other public buildings, some twenty-five in all, show the rise of architectural display from the dignity of civic Grecian at the Royal Institution (now the Royal Scottish Academy, 1834) through the showy Italian of Glasgow's Faculty of Procurators' Hall (1854) to the prodigious classical synthesis of her City Chambers (1883). Gradually civic display yields to more specialised themes of public service, still supported by style as an image-maker; Scottish gothic at the Albert Institute in Dundee (1867), graceful French renaissance at Edinburgh's Central Public Library (1887), one of the first to benefit from the pious benefactions of the Dunfermline-born American steel magnate, Andrew

Carnegie. And what about the last building in *Scotstyle*, the Burrell Gallery (1983)? Appropriately, because it is the receptacle for so much style, and because it is in Mackintosh's own city of Glasgow, it follows Mackintosh's ideal — a pure style, beyond historical quotation.

In 1834 the urbanisation of central Scotland was already gathering speed. In that year the church extension committee, with Dr Thomas Chalmers as its chairman, was set up to raise money for the building of 220 churches, mainly in the new industrial areas. But this was only a start; in the 1831 census the population of Scotland was 2.4 million and by 1931 it had doubled to 4.8 million, seven tenths of them living in towns, while the dozen predominantly agricultural counties actually had fewer inhabitants than a century before. By 1939 it had topped 5 million.

The broad pattern of Scotland's industrial growth and subsequent decline, followed by her striving for a new economic base, are well known. Agriculture, despite its decreasing workforce and a series of setbacks that began with the free trade reforms of the 1850s, has remained the most important industry in terms of land use and the most capable of adaptation to meet changing demand. *Scotstyle* includes one of the stone steadings, architect-designed in local materials, that form the most conspicuous type of rural architecture in Scotland (1872).

Other industries, less flexible, boomed and faltered, sometimes boomed again but tended eventually to bust. In textiles, cotton superseded the native flax because it was more suitable for machine processing, but suffered a fatal blow in 1861 when the American civil war cut off the supply of raw cotton. Dundee's jute industry rose and fell, leaving an even more splendid — and concentrated — heritage of buildings (see 1865). Some of the more advanced and specialised industries lived longer, like carpet-making. Templeton's exotically fronted factory (1889, now converted to a business centre) still advertises itself to Glasgow Green. But the main attraction for capital and labour in Victorian Scotland, gaining additional strength from those manufacturing industries that had already gone downhill, were the heavy operations connected with iron and steel. Over the sixty years up to the end of the 1914–18 war, iron production maintained a high level of roaring prosperity, though increasingly reliant on the import of foreign ores for steel. But heavy manufactures fluctuated wildly; shipbuilding reached a peak in the early 20th century but by 1931 it was already in a state of long-term decline. The tyre factory at Inchinnan (1930), NCR and Timex at Dundee (1946 and 1947) and Cummins at Shotts (1980) tell a tale of gradual adaptation in Scottish industry, and the increasing employment of architects to give decent order to important enterprises.

Most of the thirteen "industrial" buildings in *Scotstyle* are the products of industry rather that its workplaces. Gardner's "Iron Building" in Jamaica Street, Glasgow (1856) is world famous. There are also the great single sheds like the Royal Scottish Museum (1861) and Glasgow's Queen Street Station (1880), and sleek glazed webs like the Kibble Palace (1873) and the joyous station where trippers arrive at Wemyss Bay (1905). By that last date sixty years of railway building had given Scotland 3,500 miles of double or single track. It also generated architecture along the way, like the Atholl Palace Hydro at Pitlochry with its bluff French — not Scottish — baronial towers (1878). And it provided mobility for building materials, enlivening many a grey townscape with red sandstone from Dumfries-shire towards the end of the century. The amazing Art Nouveau skeleton of "The Hatrack" in St. Vincent Street, Glasgow (1899) would not have looked half as jolly in Giffnock stone; nor would it have stood up for so long.

Among the twenty-three commercial buildings here, some of the shops give the clearest impression of deliberate modernity. St. Cuthbert's store in Edinburgh (1937) has a plain curtain wall. Alternatively they aim at tradition; Mr Jenner and his architect went shopping in Oxford and Flanders for the creation of their image in Princes Street (1885). Office buildings, if they want to be special, tend to plump for modern — and still more modern if you look at the back elevation of Northern Assurance in Glasgow (1909). Insurance, the buildings tell us, is a matter for the present and future. So which would you prefer — the straightforward curtain wall of Standard Life (1964) or the outrageous nostalgia (apparently for Holland in the twenties) of the Scottish Provident three years later? Banks are another thing. All over Scotland, Victorian architects were commissioned to design enduring monuments and palaces of money. And they have endured, starting with the brilliant North of Scotland in Aberdeen (1839) and subsequently led by David Bryce — only the second architect I cannot resist mentioning by name — for British Linen (1851) and the Bank of Scotland (1868).

If churches seem second to banks in the hierarchy of the Scottish town, it is probably because they are now less used, but the eighteen in *Scotstyle* tell clearly of the pride with which they were built. They start with the finest of all gothic revival steeples in Britain, at the Tolbooth in Edinburgh (1844). The breakaway Free Church, formed in 1843, found its most powerful expression in the Barclay-Bruntsfield in Edinburgh (1864), the United Presbyterians at St. Vincent Street, Glasgow (1859). The Episcopalians excelled with their church — now the Cathedral — in Dundee (1853), and their lonely Cathedral and college on the isle of Cumbrae (1852); indeed their creative ecclesiology was to be emulated by the Church of Scotland well into the 20th century, as at St. Conan's by Loch Awe (1927) and the Reid Memorial Church in Edinburgh (1932). One important feature of later 20th century church architecture is that it gives the designer a chance to make a simple statement with a basically single-cell building like the church at Glenrothes (1957); but complication, with symbolic intent, can still be seen in St. Bride's Roman Catholic church at East Kilbride (1962). The problem of conservation, aggravated by the re-union of the Church of Scotland and the Free Church in 1929, presents a special challenge to architects today.

The dozen country houses in *Scotstyle* — an influential but not always conspicuous element in the Scottish scene — begin rather disconcertingly with the frowning Romanesque of Lennox Castle (1837). The baronial renaissance is represented not, as I would have expected, with David Bryce but with a much gentler soul, Patrick Allan-Fraser and his delightfully quirky Hospitalfield (1866). From the ebullient "Coll-Earn" (1866) to Robert Lorimer's highly convincing Formakin (1912) the point is firmly brought home; there is no "Scottish Baronial" stereotype except in the eye of the caricaturist or the tired critic. Mackintosh himself showed this at Hill House (1903), for which he claimed the quality of "no style"; though it is related, of course, to what is called the Scottish vernacular.

Hill House is not really a country house but a villa. Mackintosh owed a lot to his Alexander Thomson scholarship, and "Greek" Thomson himself was the greatest of our Victorian villa designers. His extraordinary Grecian manner, which has an ancestor at "The Vine", Dundee (1836), came to full fruition at "Holmwood" (1858). This in turn can be compared and contrasted with modern villas of studied informality like "Avisfield" in Edinburgh (1958).

Finally there are the twenty-odd examples of "community housing". Of course it had the Georgian record of success in the background, but it took this record a lot further. Edinburgh's Victorian achievement is good enough, but Glasgow's planned developments for prosperous magnates and professional people keep up the old Georgian discipline with notable brilliance at Kirklee Terrace (1846) and the Park development (1855), not to mention Thomson's solemn magnificence at Great Western Terrace (1869). Later on, I would have liked to see some acknowledgement of those rough-topped baronial tenements for the lower middle class in which Edinburgh managed to excel even Glasgow; and something of the pioneer work of James Gowans, the obsessive technician who had a real interest in working class housing. Honour is paid, however, to Patrick Geddes whose Ramsay Garden (1893) shows him as a real enhancer and preserver of the town's fabric. The phrase he used was "conservative surgery".

Public authority housing, and the massive problem posed by the huge backlog of makeshift and inadequate housing stock, is a Scottish problem that was tackled on a national scale by a succession of housing acts but never had a national solution. With hindsight we now see that small solutions were good ones; The Inch scheme to the south of Edinburgh (1949) turned out better than the mixed and high-rise housing ghettoes that followed. Too often the architects failed to tell the politicians what would go wrong, and bad detailing, bad maintenance and bad management did the rest. The most recent housing in *Scotstyle* is the charming riverside development at Bridgend, Perth (1978) — old-fashioned low rise. But is there still something to learn about the detailing of concrete blockwork — especially at wall-heads?

Looking at *Scotstyle's* period as a whole, it is obviously wrong to ignore the disasters and continuing failures, from which a lot could be learned. But it is equally important to remember how many of Scotland's environmental assets have come down to us from these 150 years or been handed on to us from earlier times. First, though large tracts of the lowlands have been blighted by industrial sprawl, its concentration has resulted in a very large area remaining unspoiled. Then we owe a lot to the tradition of discipline; certainly to the discipline imposed till quite recently by the character of native building materials, but also to the continuance of the old system of feudal control by landlords. This has been largely replaced by the development controls imposed by local authorities and the state (including listed building control), all of which are frequently and bitterly criticized. Would the colourful and very un-Scottish development at Ramsay Garden, near the summit of Edinburgh's castle rock, (1893), be given planning consent (including the necessary consent for building in an outstanding conservation area) if it were proposed today? Yes, I think it would, but equally I know that strict observance of small rules can produce results that are wasteful or laughable. Controls are a safety-net, not a design tool.

Most of all, we are indebted to another Scottish trait which persisted at least to the 1930s and is now (assisted, one hopes, by the Festival of Architecture) reviving; the tradition of investing in solid, good-looking architecture. For tangible return? Long-term economy? For personal or corporate prestige, or from public spirit? All these may have something to do with it, and are reflected in Scotland's present stock of good buildings.

Finally, what about the architect himself? He is or should be, as *Scotstyle* shows, much more than a mere stylist. Bruce, Adam and Mackintosh illustrate the point — all of them abundantly stylish, but in the end it is not the style that impresses. Scottish architects are particularly good at assimilating influences from the past or from abroad, doing it in the only real way, which is by keen observation and careful recording. But the main point is that so many of them have been able to produce buildings which do their job and speak to us, ultimately, not out of a history book or a travel brochure but just for themselves.

All of which demands a postscript. After a hundred and fifty years in which architects have acquired and consolidated their professional status, they are now more than ever aware of the awesome responsibility of their job. Are they going to delegate more of it? Are they going to find themselves bowing out of everything except drawing shapes on paper and perhaps being allowed to chair the building design team? I hope not. Or if they are, we shall have to invent, for the management of this whole complicated business, some sort of genius who knows about function and construction and visual delight, and the way they ought to work together, and can at the same time be a leader. Somebody, in short, rather like an architect.

1834

The Royal Scottish Academy, Princes Street, Edinburgh
William Henry Playfair

The first phase of Edinburgh's Royal Scottish Academy of Painting, Sculpture and Architecture, then known as the Royal Institution, was completed in 1826, but with accommodation which was rendered inadequate after barely five years in use. In his capacity as the architect of the original scheme, William Playfair was invited to prepare plans for its enlargement, despite the recommendations of one of his colleagues that "the present Building should be taken down". Certainly, the subsequent alterations — commenced in 1832 and completed three years later — substantially transformed the original structure and now, with the addition of Sir John Steell's statue of Queen Victoria perched atop the Princes Street facade, the RSA is as impressive as befits one of the few buildings whose erection was permitted on the south side of the thoroughfare. It is made all the more rich and sturdy through comparison with the neighbouring National Gallery, built to Playfair's designs in 1845. While the former is a great, Grecian ponderous mass resplendent with incised ornament, scrolls and wreaths, the later building is relatively unadorned, slim and elegant — essentially a feminine composition sited alongside a bolder, altogether more hearty building. This meeting on the Mound of the Doric and Ionic Orders has given Edinburgh two fine city landmarks.

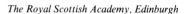

The Royal Scottish Academy, Edinburgh

1835

Inverness Castle, Castle Wynd, Inverness
William Burn/Thomas Brown

Inverness Castle currently houses the town's Sheriff Court complex and Police headquarters. It comprises two huge castellated blocks — dissimilar but not ill-matched — one a relatively formal building with a heavily buttressed entrance, the other a picturesque cluster of assorted towers. The two are linked by a perimeter wall along which are featured bartizans and towers. This, and the associated buildings behind, are characterised by a pinky-red sandstone, which looks well set high above the grassy slopes of the east bank of the Ness. The

Inverness Castle, Inverness

development was begun around 1833, at which time construction was commenced on the older of the two buildings, to replace the original castle which lay in a near ruinous state close by. This block, low and with squared and circular towers, was designed by William Burn of Edinburgh, and completed in 1836. Ten years later, the adjacent prison block was begun to designs by Thomas Brown. The massing of this second building is altogether more imposing, although several features apparent in the earlier work have been retained. Thus, the repetition of corbelled parapets, string coursing and single and tripled windows lends the scheme a collective identity.

'The Vine', Dundee

1836

'The Vine', 43 Magdalen Yard Road, Dundee
Architect unknown

'The Vine', Dundee

Nestling behind a screen of trees on a corner site on the outskirts of Dundee's Magdalen Green is a compact little villa whose detailing is of Greek origin but the disposition of which is particularly unusual. 'The Vine' was built in 1836 as a residence and private art gallery for George Duncan MP, whose original collection is now housed in the City Art Gallery. The building is low, rectangular on plan with a semi-basement, and comprising a series of rooms grouped around a central hall. This is lit by an attractive timber and glazed cupola which is barely visible above the shallow, slated roof. The entrance is located at the east end of the house, flanked on either side by chubby Doric columns and with a strange blank pediment above. A similar pediment appears on the slightly protruding central bay of the south elevation, where the facade is dominated by the seemingly disproportionately large pylon-like windows. These have blank panels below and some highly decorative wreath work above. A series of shallow terraces to the south lend the building stature as steps fall away to the lawn beyond.

Lennox Castle, Lennoxtown

1837

Lennox Castle, Lennoxtown
David Hamilton

Begun in 1837, Lennox Castle was designed towards the close of David Hamilton's career. The "recognised head of the profession", he was in his late sixties when approached by J L Kincaid-Lennox to design an extensive addition to the mansion of Woodhead, the family seat in the parish of Campsie. Plans were in preparation when Kincaid-Lennox, who longed to resurrect the ancient title of Earl of Lennox, was persuaded to finance the construction of a new house, to be built in a style redolent of "the early origin of the family, in the period of the Norman Conquest". A handsome and conspicuous structure, the castle was completed within four years — the north, and entrance, front comprising a bulky, buttressed, arched and battlemented porch hauled out from the base of a tall, stout tower, and flanked on either side by lower, rather busy wings with elegant pilastered corners. Woodhead, thus abandoned, but not unwanted, was partially demolished and the resultant ruin carefully decorated with climbing plants and ivy.

Library, Taymouth Castle, Perthshire

Kenmore Square, Perthshire

Dairy, Taymouth Castle, Perthshire

1838

Taymouth Castle, Kenmore, Perthshire (associated work)
James Gillespie Graham

The grounds of Taymouth Castle, formerly the chief seat of the Campbells of Breadalbane and now a Civil Defence school under the guardianship of the Home Office, are littered with strange romantic follies and gazebo-like structures. There is a curious white-harled tower with semi-castellated outhouses, a fine wrought-iron bridge, and an incredible dairy building of unknown authorship — the walls framed out in knotty timber posts between which is packed a skin of quartz and slate. Then there is the gateway to the castle, built by the clerk of works on the estate, James Smith, in 1838; a dainty, rather Disneyesque, but very fetching, Gothic composition sitting somewhat snootily at one end of the lovely square of Kenmore. The castle itself, which had survived major alterations and extensions three times over by 1839, was furnished with its most elaborate set of interiors around the same time as the construction of the gateway, when James Gillespie Graham was approached by the second Marquess to make alterations to the west wing of the house. The library — in the design of which Gillespie Graham is generally reckoned to have leaned heavily on the expertise and assistance of A W N Pugin — is a staggeringly rich space; profuse in its use of intricate carving with the handsome timberwork much highlighted by the delicate use of gilding. It was "furnished with all that luxury can desire or wealth bestow". Both castle and contents were auctioned off in 1922 but the house, grounds and approach have succeeded in retaining most of their romantic appeal.

Gates, Taymouth Castle, Perthshire

14

1839

North of Scotland Bank, 5 Castle Street, Aberdeen
Archibald Simpson

Alongside that of John Smith, Simpson's name is that most closely associated with the architectural development of the Granite City during the first half of the nineteenth century. He was fortunate indeed to have at his disposal the great wealth of hard grey granite from the nearby Rubislaw quarry. Certainly, the North of Scotland Bank — now the Clydesdale Bank — is enhanced by a clarity and precision which would no doubt have been lost by now had it been built in sandstone. The building stands on the obtuse junction of Castle Street and King Street, cleverly manoeuvring the corner with a quadrant Corinthian portico above which sits a terracotta sculpture group designed by James Giles and featuring Ceres, the goddess of plenty. Despite the pronounced channelling of the stonework and the strong horizontal line created by the second storey cornice, the accent is on verticality, particularly at the corner where slender columns frame a single, tall doorway in the curving wall behind. It is a serene building, spoiled only fractionally by the painting of the terracotta sculpture and by the renewal of some of the windows. Internally, however, it is as gloriously rich as when first opened in October 1842 — still complete with gilt Parthenon frieze, Corinthian pilasters and superb ornamental plasterwork.

North of Scotland Bank, Aberdeen

1840

The Scott Monument, Princes Street, Edinburgh
George Meikle Kemp

The capital city has no shortage of fantastic monuments. Of these, the Scott Monument in Princes Street soars up and out of its surround of lush foliage to challenge the very best. Built to the competition-winning designs of the self-

The Scott Monument, Edinburgh

taught "architect" George Meikle Kemp — who submitted his scheme under the pseudonym of a medieval mason — it is a Gothic fantasy, a romantic pile constructed during a predominantly classical period in the city's architectural development. It is a proud and fitting tribute to one of Scotland's most famous sons, an elongated composition of pinnacles upon pillars, arches and buttresses, indents and niches — the whole fairly dripping with gothic ornament. It is also something of a monument to the designer, who stumbled into a canal one evening barely eight months before the building's completion and drowned. The statue of Sir Walter Scott, designed and executed by Sir John Steell, was installed in 1846 in time for the formal inauguration of the monument on August 15th, six years to the day on which the foundation stone had been laid.

The Blythswood Testimonial, Renfrew

Donaldson's Hospital, Edinburgh

1841

The Blythswood Testimonial, Blythswood Road, Renfrew
John Stephen

John Stephen preceded Alexander Thomson, James Sellars and Alexander Skirving in a progression of Glasgow architects who perpetuated the Greek Revival style in architecture long after its popularity had been exhausted elsewhere. His scheme for what was known as the Renfrew Grammar School and Blythswood Testimonial was selected for construction as a monument to Archibald Campbell of Blythswood, who had died in June 1838 after many years of prominence in the locality. The school is cruciform in plan with two single-storey classroom wings of undressed ashlar abutting the main, two-storey body of the building, similarly constructed and housing additional classrooms and the headmaster's quarters above. Fronting this is a striking entrance facade which features an unusual three-tiered tower and modest Doric portico. The central section of the tower is clearly inspired by the Choragic Monument of Lysicrates in Athens, with the upper and lower sections less obviously derived but equally Grecian in origin. While the combination of tiered steeple and portico can be most closely traced to St. Pancras in London (1819–1822), the proportions and juxtaposition of elements are Stephen's own. While this main elevation is in relatively good condition, however, the remainder of the building — particularly the wings with their pylon-like entrances — is structurally suspect. It has ceased to function as a school, and may soon cease to serve as a monument also.

1842

Donaldson's Hospital, Haymarket Terrace, Edinburgh
William Henry Playfair

Two miles west of Edinburgh's Princes Street is sited the former Donaldson's Hospital, William Playfair's architectural homage to the splendid Tudor and Jacobean mansions of late sixteenth and early seventeenth century England. Set on a vast, smooth, grassy plain, the building — now a school for the deaf, and an oasis in its setting — is a crowded collection of verticals; tall mullioned windows, high octagonal entrance turrets, chimneys, buttresses, finials and square corner towers. As if this were not sufficient, the walls are further decorated with bay windows, hood moulds and a wealth of intricate strapwork. Built with funds left by James Donaldson, an Edinburgh printer, this quadrangular complex cost £100,000 to complete. It was constructed between 1842 and 1854.

Trinity College, Glenalmond

1843

Trinity College, Glenalmond
John Henderson

The notion of establishing a college in Scotland for the purpose of training young men for the Ministry, and at the same time providing an education for sons of the gentry, first occurred to William Gladstone in 1840, shortly before his appointment as Vice-President of the Board of Trade under Peel's Government. Together with his friend and contemporary James Hope-Scott, he secured the tentative support of the College of Bishops and spent the autumn of 1842 travelling around Perthshire in search of a suitable site. Part of the estate of Cairnies in Glenalmond — "in the neighbourhood of wild and open country" — was selected, and the Edinburgh architect John Henderson instructed to prepare plans. Building work, begun in 1843, proceeded slowly, and of the planned quadrangle only the north entrance facade and the adjoining west wing were completed in time for the opening ceremony. These were built using the deep red sandstone quarried close to the site, and are in the style of the Elizabethan period in English Renaissance architecture. The north elevation has an arched entrance flanked on either side by buttresses, while the walls which extend out from the central tower are enlivened by stout chimneys expressed through the full height of the building. Further additions, as they could be afforded, were made to the complex by Henderson, Sir G G Scott and Andrew Heiton of Perth. Finally, in 1926, the school's founder was commemorated in the construction of the Gladstone cloister.

1844

Tolbooth St. John's Church, Castlehill, Edinburgh
Jame Gillespie Graham with A W N Pugin

Tolbooth St. John's Church, Edinburgh

The bulky outline of the Tolbooth St. John's Church guards the approach to Edinburgh Castle — solid and reassuring with an impressive pinnacled tower and slim, octagonal spire; the tallest in Edinburgh at 73 metres high. Built as the Victoria Hall to house the Tolbooth congregation and the General Assembly of the Church of Scotland, it has an unusual interior with a ground floor central corridor leading to a fine imperial staircase at the west end. This rises into the auditorium space above — galleried and with tiered seating. Designed in the mid-pointed English Gothic style, the architects of the church were James Gillespie Graham and Augustus Welby Northmore Pugin. Pugin, shipwrecked off Leith in 1830, was a highly influential protagonist in the promotion of Gothic forms — persuasively arguing a return to the principles of early fourteenth century 'Pointed' architecture in a series of books, of which the first published was *Contrasts* (1836). He found a sympathetic partner in Gillespie Graham, just as he did in Sir Charles Barry with whom he collaborated on the competition-winning scheme for the Houses of Parliament (1839–1852). Here, Pugin was responsible for most of the internal detail, just as the intricate timberwork on the interior of the Edinburgh church was executed to his designs by William Nixon. The church is now vacant, the congregation having moved to the Greyfriars Kirk.

1845

The Royal College of Physicians' Hall, 9 Queen Street, Edinburgh
Thomas Hamilton

Granted their first Royal Charter in 1681 by Charles II, the members of Edinburgh's Royal College of Physicians were obliged to meet in a series of temporary buildings until 1781, at which time they were able to occupy their first purpose-built headquarters in George Street. These were erected to the designs of James Craig — architect of the city's New Town. 1843, however, found the College in debt, and the speedy sale of the building had to be negotiated, thus allowing the members to purchase a small terraced house in Queen Street. Thomas Hamilton was appointed to prepare plans to replace the house with new premises of "some architectural pretensions". He responded with a Graeco-Roman composition, richer internally than out, but nonetheless achieving a dignified and impressive frontage — protruding slightly beyond its neighbours and boasting a fine tiered, pedimented entrance portico. Clearly, the most outstanding feature of the facade is this centrepiece. The ground floor portico is supported on columns derived from the Tower of the Winds in

Athens. That on the first floor is flanked and surmounted by three classical figures — statues portraying Hygeia, Aesculapius and Hippocrates. Proportionally, the composition has little in common with either of its Georgian neighbours, with elongated first floor windows above which the stonework fails to act as either frieze or third storey, but which nevertheless provides a horizontal element powerful enough to balance the verticality of the centrepiece. The restraint of the entrance elevation does little to prepare one for the extravagance of the entrance hall and staircase within. These remain much the same as when detailed by Hamilton, although the meeting hall to the rear of the building was more than doubled in 1865, by David Bryce, who also added the splendid library.

The Royal College of Physicians' Hall, Edinburgh

Kirklee Terrace, Glasgow

Kirklee Terrace, Great Western Road, Glasgow
Charles Wilson

Glasgow's spacious West End expanded during the early 1840s in an attempt to accommodate the growth of the city's upper middle-class. Of the twenty-three estates whose formation was designed to achieve this, Kelvinside — covering 576 acres — was the largest. It was the Kelvinside Estate Company who shrewdly feued part of their land to the Royal Botanic Institution, whose plants and glasshouse were transferred in 1842 to their present home close to Great Western Road. With what was then a private pleasure ground in a prime location, the company appointed Charles Wilson to commence work on the design of a series of "dwelling houses of superior description" immediately adjacent to the gardens. High Windsor Terrace, as it was first known, represents one of Wilson's earliest essays in the grand Italianate style, and a splendid attempt it was, albeit only revealed as such as late as 1864, when the last houses were completed. In its elevated position, hidden for the most part behind dense trees, the terrace is a compilation of meticulous details. Windows are surrounded by bold architraves which give rise to sturdy consoles supporting simple cornices. Entrance porches support weighty balconies, the circular detail on which is cunningly repeated in miniature above the windows. The centrepiece and terminal projections of the building are a storey higher and slightly advanced, and the gable ends superbly articulated. This, then, was the stylish, energetic, palatial example set by one of Glasgow's most talented Victorian architects to those of his successors who were given the opportunity to design some of the many fine terraces which line Great Western Road. Only Alexander Thomson was able to surpass the example.

1847

Bank of Scotland, 9–11 High Street, Inverness
MacKenzie and Matthews

Crowded on either side by two featureless four storey blocks, the High Street branch of the Bank of Scotland in Inverness is imbued with a perennial poise which sets it apart from the buildings around. An impressive terminal feature to the length of Castle Street, it was originally built as the headquarters of the Caledonian Bank by the architect Thomas MacKenzie of Elgin and his partner James Matthews. It rapidly dissociates itself from the buildings between which it is caught through the recession of the upper two storeys, centred on which is an ornate pediment with sculptured figures by Handyside Ritchie. This is raised above four elegant Corinthian columns which rest on channelled ashlar piers below. The ground floor — advanced to follow the building line — is thus subdivided into five bays, of which the outer two are wider and contain arched doorways. Of these, both have wrought-iron gates and one a richly sculpted tympanum. The recession of the upper two floors creates a balcony at first floor window level, at either end of which sit huge decorative urns on which are depicted Queen Victoria and the Prince Consort. Additional decoration, while confined to specific areas, is extremely rich — with elaborate carved swags featured in the panels between first and second floor windows. It is interesting to compare this building with David Bryce's British Linen Bank in Edinburgh (1851), the treatment of which is similar.

Bank of Scotland, Inverness

Ardnamurchan Lighthouse, Plan

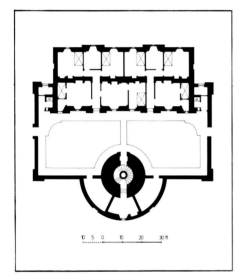

1848

Ardnamurchan Lighthouse, Ardnamurchan
Alan Stevenson

Scotland's first lighthouse was constructed on the Isle of May in 1636, built from local rubble and with a vaulted, flagstone roof on which burned a brazier of lighted coals. With the exception of this, and a few subsequent local beacons and lights, mariners had little to guide them through hazardous waters until the formation of the Northern Lighthouse Board in 1786. Stevenson, uncle of the writer Robert Louis, succeeded his father as engineer to the board in 1843. Ardnamurchan was lighted in 1849, by which time the principles of lighthouse construction had so developed that greater thought could be given to decorating the fabric of the building. In common with most mainland beacons, the tower itself is closely linked to a ground level collection of rooms and stores. The layout is symmetrical and the detailing precise — from the pylon-like entrance doorway at the base of the tower, to the graceful corbelling of the stonework beneath the lantern. Even the chimneys are stately little squared miniatures of the tower! While the complex has been rudely extended to the rear, it still presents a majestic facade to the sea — one of the last great stone-built lighthouses of the period. Shortly after Ardnamurchan was completed, brick, timber and iron, being easier to transport and handle than stone, became the primary building materials for Scotland's coastal beacons.

1849

The Hamilton Mausoleum, Hamilton
David Bryce

The Hamilton Mausoleum, Hamilton

Two enormous stone lions — one watchful and alert, the other slumbering peacefully — sprawl atop the entrance facade to the crypt of the Hamilton Palace Mausoleum. Above and behind them soars the imposing mass of the funerary chapel — a vigorously modelled stone drum seated on a high square podium and finishing in a smooth-cheeked dome, featureless but for the single glazed oculus which lights the space within. Beneath this solemn structure lies the crypt. The Mausoleum was erected within sight of the now vanished Hamilton Palace for Alexander, the 10th Duke, who originally lay in the chapel itself, sealed inside an Egyptian sarcophagus which he had purchased in Paris on behalf of the British Museum, but which he later secured for his own use. The Duke was highly influential in determining the overall appearance of the building, with David Bryce of Edinburgh, who succeeded to the commission on the death of Glasgow's David Hamilton, finalising the proposals, which included a severe Roman Renaissance interior. The chapel, however, was never consecrated as such once it was discovered that the chamber produced awesome echoes which could last for anything up to fifteen seconds. This phenomenon serves to intensify the funereal aura of the space which, without the extraordinary amount of light which streams down the coffered face of the dome to illuminate the marble mosaic floor, would be overpowering. Evidence of settlement was detected in the structure around 1921, at which time the crypt began to flood and the coffins and sarcophagus were removed to the family plot in the nearby Bent Cemetery.

1850

The Neilson Institute, Paisley
Charles Wilson

With but few exceptions, Paisley's most distinctive architecture is to be found concentrated in the area which surrounds the Oakshaw Hill. Here are sited Hippolyte Jean Blanc's outrageously bombastic Coats Memorial Church

The Neilson Institute, Paisley

(1894), the elegant little Coats Observatory (1884) by John Honeyman, and Charles Wilson's John Neilson Endowment School, begun in 1849 and now known as the Neilson Institute. This last building, erected as it was on the crest of the hill, dominates the skyline— its lead covered dome combining well with the numerous towers and spires around to create an exciting and varied city silhouette, the effect of which is visible for miles around. The school, opened on April 5th 1852, originally comprised four classrooms around a central hall. This hall, timber panelled and floored and reached by a long, barrel-vaulted entrance corridor, is lit by the glass topped dome — the unusual truncated outline of which greatly relieves an otherwise severely neoclassical exterior. Certainly the dome is less typical of Wilson's work than, say, the semi-circular

The British Linen Company's Bank, Edinburgh

headed windows which light the classrooms. It grows up and out of a stone drum, which in turn is supported on an octagonal base centred squarely on the entrance portico and featuring four corner tripods bearing ornamental vases. The dome was readily accepted as a fitting tribute to the school's founder, and the school described in a Government report as "most ample, commodious and elegant". Notwithstanding its many virtues, the building was closed in 1977, its doors and windows bricked up and the facade vandalised. At the time of writing, its future is uncertain.

1851

The British Linen Company's Bank, St. Andrew Square, Edinburgh
David Bryce

Designed by David Bryce in 1846, and largely completed by 1851, Edinburgh's British Linen Bank — now an office of the Bank of Scotland — was less than enthusiastically reported in a contemporary journal, where it was felt that "more should have been made of it". It is difficult to imagine how. No doubt the construction cost of £30,000 seemed excessive at the time, but the building has weathered well and readily lends itself to much more favourable criticism today. The entrance facade, sandwiched as it is between two rather more sombre buildings, is an elaborate neo-Roman composition — the somewhat squat nature of the proportions more than adequately counteracted by six fluted Corinthian columns which, detached from the main body of the elevation, rise through the upper two storeys to be surmounted by huge statues representing Agriculture, Mechanics, Architecture, Industry, Commerce and Navigation. The entablature which winds its way between and around these columns is particularly rich, as is the sculpture which appears in the tympana above the first floor windows. The ground floor and semi-basement are heavily rusticated, providing a solid base for the more ornate work above. The interior is equally sumptuous, with a cruciform shaped telling-room lit by a coffered cupola, a splendid mosaic floor and polished granite columns which cost £1,000 each.

1852

The Cathedral of the Isles, Millport, Great Cumbrae Island
William Butterfield

The Cathedral of the Isles, Millport

Gladstone's success in establishing the Trinity College at Glenalmond (1843) inspired the Hon. George F Boyle to plan a similar venture on a smaller scale and of a wholly ecclesiastical nature on his estate on the Great Cumbrae Island near Bute. The scheme did not properly materialise, but the Cathedral of the Isles at Millport was subsequently begun by Boyle in 1849, and built with adjacent Provost's house, dormitory, and choir with cloisters to designs by the English architect William Butterfield. Butterfield was an active practitioner of the doctrines of the Oxford Movement, who sought a revival of the Church of England through a return to the practices of early Christianity. Being of a related faith, the style adopted for this Episcopalian church was of an appropriately simple and dignified Gothic Revival architecture, executed in a local stone and Ballachulish slate, and with a minimum of applied decoration — paved flooring, painted oak beams and some stained glass. The proportions of the church are deceptive, with the whole complex, including the Provost's house to the south, contained within the shape of a small cross. The buildings are heavily buttressed with steeply pitched roofs, and this — coupled with the fall of the site — lends the church a lofty and imposing air. It is, in fact, the smallest cathedral in Britain, seating only one hundred and twenty people.

1853

St. Paul's Episcopal Cathedral, Castlehill, Dundee
Sir George Gilbert Scott

Modelled on the fifteenth century church tower of Dundee, the tower and spire of St. Paul's Cathedral on Castlehill dominate their immediate surroundings — visible, even, from the opposite bank of the Tay, almost one and a half miles away. Once described as "an edifice to boast of" the building, while fairly handsome, is much hampered by its awkward location. Designed by Sir G G Scott for Alexander Penrose Forbes, the Bishop of Brechin, the church was erected on the site of the ancient castle of Dundee. It is in the mid-Decorated Gothic style and comprises a nave with side aisles, with each bay expressed externally in the manner of separate gables, a choir with side chapels, and a semi-octagonal apse at the east end — the masonry vaults over which were the most ambitious to be undertaken in Scotland at the time. Internally, the high altar features a mosaic reredos by Salviati of Venice. Scott later secured the commission for the town's Albert Institute (1867).

St. Paul's Episcopal Cathedral, Dundee

1854

The Royal Faculty of Procurators' Hall, 62–68 West George Street, Glasgow
Charles Wilson

Wilson was known to respond best to commissions in his native city, where he was instrumental in popularising a revival in the Italian Renaissance style. His architecture is almost always marked by a pleasing rhythmic quality and bold use of sculpture and well tooled stonework. He was invited to submit a design for the Royal Faculty of Procurators' Hall after the London architect J T Emmett had his proposals rejected. Wilson's scheme was duly constructed in 1854, and despite undeniable similarities to the sixteenth century Venetian palace type, is in essence as Victorian as it is Italianate, all at once both exuberant and dignified. Currently painted a shade of cream, the elaborate friezework and finely fluted columns have a remarkable plasticity, all of which greatly enhances the sculptural effect of the composition. The interiors — in their original decorative state — were as rich as the exterior, the library subdivided by a series of arches supported on square columns painted to resemble marble, and the high staircase hall also arched and very fine. The sculpture, both inside and out, was executed by Alexander Handyside Ritchie, whose lawlord keystones depict prominent legal figures of the period.

The Royal Faculty of Procurators' Hall, Glasgow

ELEVATION   TO   THE   SOUTH

1855

The Park Circus Development, Woodlands Hill, Glasgow
Charles Wilson

Glasgow's West End Park — now known as Kelvingrove — was formally constituted in 1852 by the purchase of the lands of Kelvingrove and Woodlands. With a view to recouping some proportion of what had been a massive outlay, the Town Council reserved the right to build upper middle-class residences on the crest of Woodlands Hill, a rocky outcrop on whose gentle east slope had already been built a series of fine terraced houses. Charles Wilson was appointed to oversee the architectural aspect of the development, collaborating with Sir Joseph Paxton on the layout of the park itself. Of the major components of the scheme as built — Gardens, Terrace, Circus and Quadrant — Park Terrace is the most clearly visible from the grassy incline below; marching imperiously around the crest of the hill, fiercely protective of the mild mannered Circus within. The curve of the facade is punctuated at frequent intervals by slightly protruding sections with steep mansard roofs and two storey bay windows. Elsewhere there are small, round-headed dormers peeping out from the roof slope. Within, lies Park Circus, introverted and refined — decorative, but without the brashness of the Terrace, the three arms of the concave facade stretching leisurely around a small cluster of central trees. Wilson's unusual Lombardic Free Church College of 1856 and J T Rochead's Park Church of 1857 completed the scenario on the hill, a grand scheme ambitiously conceived and skilfully executed — something of a highpoint in the town planning achievements of Victorian Britain.

The Park Circus Development, Glasgow

1856

Gardner's ('The Iron Building'), 36 Jamaica Street, Glasgow
John Baird I

At the time of the construction of Gardner's furniture warehouse in Jamaica Street, glass and iron — although by no means new materials — were becoming increasingly popular as a means to an aesthetic, as well as a structural end. As early as 1827, the architect of the warehouse, John Baird I, had already incorporated a fully glazed roof supported on an iron frame in his design for the Argyle Arcade in Glasgow. Here, at Jamaica Street, the use of the iron frame is much bolder — externally exposed with the bones of the building laid bare for all to see. Long regarded as a pioneering achievement, the facade of Gardner's is skeletal indeed, but with considerable poise and wholly classical in proportional terms with each of the four floors slightly shorter than that below. The Jamaica Street frontage is constructed on a four bay module, each separated from its neighbour by a substantial iron stanchion with a slightly decorative vertical indent. Each bay is in turn subdivided into five lights, fully arched on the top floor and marginally flatter on the lower storeys. The ground floor is weightier, but only fractionally so, with the lettering above both it and the first floor appropriately neat and unassuming. Baird worked on the building in close conjunction with Robert McConnel, an ironfounder who held patents for the malleable ironwork used in the construction. The successful completion of Gardner's prompted future exercises in this idiom in the city centre, although none bettered the grace and elegance of this timeless building.

'The Iron Building', Glasgow

1857

Loch Vennachar Sluice House, Loch Vennachar, near Callander
John Frederic Bateman

Loch Vennachar lies to the east of Loch Katrine, and is overlooked from the north by Ben Ledi and bounded on the south by the stretch of the Menteith Hills. Under the 1855 Act of Parliament which established the supply of water to the City of Glasgow, a maximum of 50 million gallons could be drawn from Katrine in any one day. At the same time, however, 40 million gallons had to be discharged into the River Teith, and so Vennachar, and the smaller Loch Drunkie, became compensation reservoirs to meet this demand. A great masonry dam constructed in a solemn neo-classical style was created at the natural eastern outlet of Loch Vennachar, featuring a range of cast-iron sluices which facilitated control of the water level. Set on a deep stone podium with eleven arched openings of differing widths, the main body of the building is long, low and dignified, with the only concession to frivolity being the coloured glass used in the centre of each window panel. Three bays, one at either end and the other in a central position, are slightly advanced, higher and with shallow pediments. The stone is rough hewn but regular, the roof constructed of simple stone slabs supported on closely centred cast-iron trusses. Surrounded as it is by lush, rolling countryside where buildings are few and far between, this handsome little structure is a pleasant and unexpected feature of the landscape. Particularly attractive are the elaborate stone salmon ladders which permit fish to pass unimpeded in and out of the loch.

Loch Vennachar Sluice House, Loch Vennachar

'Holmwood', Cathcart, Glasgow

1858

'Holmwood', Netherlee Road, Cathcart, Glasgow
Alexander Thomson

The architectural achievements of Alexander Thomson far surpassed those of any of his immediate contemporaries, so wholly original was his interpretation of Greek and Egyptian forms — his style quite without precedent and impossible to emulate successfully. 'Holmwood', now the Convent of Our Lady of the Missions, is the most elaborate of his Glasgow built villas — a wealth of spectacularly fresh ideas clearly evident both internally and out. The entrance facade is composed of a series of elements, each effortlessly yet inextricably bound together, each material accomplishing a particular purpose, each detail assigned a specific place. Glazing and timber are secondary to the stonework of the facade, decorative certainly, but essentially functional, incidental to the overall pattern of the elevation. This is most clearly and dramatically demonstrated in the curving bay window at ground floor level, where the slender stone columns supporting a hefty cornice above stand well clear of the windows passing behind. The low, spreading eaves of the shallow roofs increase the horizontality of the composition, already elongated through the inclusion of a low stone wall and coachhouse in the principal elevation. Internally, the house is richly decorated with elaborate friezes, ornamental plasterwork and Egypto-Greek doorways. The main staircase is lit by a splendid cupola, and there is the unexpected and ingenious provision of rooflighting over the original location of the dining-room sideboard. Thomson's attention to detail was meticulous, his sense of colour lively, his use of classical ornament profuse and his style unique. His was an individual architecture — and as such immeasurably precious.

St. Vincent Street Free Church, Glasgow

1859

St. Vincent Street Free Church, 265 St. Vincent Street, Glasgow
Alexander Thomson

The asymmetrical grouping of elevated temple facade and tower was the unusual device used to good effect on two of the three Glasgow churches built to the designs of Alexander Thomson. Of these two (the third, the Queen's Park UP Church (1867) no longer remains) only the St. Vincent Street Free Church is still in use. A disastrous fire in October 1965 gutted the former Caledonia Road UP Church (1856) and only walls and tower are left. Opened on February 20th 1859, the St. Vincent Street building is an incredible bag of mixed motifs — a Grecian temple with galleried aisles terminating in strange Egyptian pylons resting on a mammoth stone podium, out of which also rises a square stone tower topped by an elongated dome of unusual origin. Thomson used the podium, which actually houses the main body of the church with halls below, to absorb the steep slope of the site. The 'temple' therefore, houses not the church so much as it does the galleries and upper section of the main hall, a layout not quite suggested by the composition of the exterior. The tower, linked briefly at its base to the remainder of the building, is a magnificent totem-pole of an affair — square for the most part, briefly octagonal, and round thereafter — stretching languorously to a point beneath an ornamental urn. The cumulative effect of the many curious elements displayed at the top of this spire is quite unique — an amalgam of details which combines to produce a composite whole without serious rival in terms of originality, complexity and sheer audacity.

1860

The National Wallace Monument, Abbey Craig, Stirling
John Thomas Rochead

It is much more a measure of the architect's not inconsiderable output than it is of the city's ability to preserve its Victorian heritage that Glasgow can still

The National Wallace Monument, Stirling

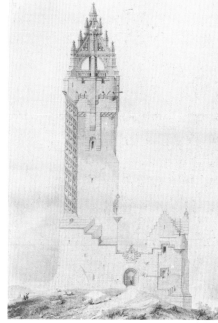

boast a number of very fine works by J T Rochead. None, however, can compare with the stirring spectacle that is the National Wallace Monument in Stirling. This building is exciting to behold and a delight to experience at close hand, whether it is through the long haul up the sides of the basaltic Abbey Craig from where only glimpses can be had until the summit is reached, or through the dizzying climb up the tight spiral staircase to the platform beneath the crown tower from where expansive panoramas unfold of the Scottish Lowlands. Rochead's liberal use of Scottish Baronial detailing could at times be disturbingly enthusiastic, but here the detail is rich but restrained, unusual and occasionally inappropriate, but combining to produce a great, glorious, patriotic mass. The 220 foot high freestone tower comprises a vertical procession of four vast barrel-vaulted chambers, the ground floor housing an audio-visual display, the other three more ancient memorabilia. The climb to the top, up the externally expressed staircase, is rewarded by the awesome sight of the culminating pinnacles above and the spectacular views beyond. The monument took over eight years to complete.

The Royal Scottish Museum, Edinburgh

1861

The Royal Scottish Museum, Chambers Street, Edinburgh
Captain Francis Fowke

Were the splendid exhibits not reason enough to visit Edinburgh's Royal Scottish Museum, a positive bonus is to be had in simple appreciation of the very fine interior. Wrapped in a grave sandstone facade — a Tuscan villa of some charm but which gives little indication of the structure within — this building perfectly typifies the effect which could be created using the engineering materials which the Victorians sought to exploit. Slender cast-iron columns are in abundance here, supporting at the one level the peripheral timber balconies which characterise the main spaces and, at the other level, arched timber ribs upon which are carried copiously glazed roofs. Designed by Captain Fowke of the Royal Engineers, the building was erected in three phases, commencing in 1861 and substantially completed by 1888. The lofty entrance hall — an interior space of considerable elegance — has been harmed little by subsequent additions and alterations to the complex. The lower lengths of the cast-iron columns were replaced in steel in 1954, and a handsome travertine floor laid in 1970. Really, about the only disappointing feature of this uplifting interior is that visitors are not permitted to guddle the goldfish lazing in the ornamental pools!

Fettes College, Edinburgh

1862

Fettes College, East Fettes Avenue, Edinburgh
David Bryce

Bryce was a prolific and accomplished architect, but one whose classical work was occasionally overindulgent and whose Scottish-Baronial exercises could at times be overblown. Fettes College contrives to be both, despite and as a result of which it is a thoroughly enjoyable building — romantic, exotic and unrestrained. Designed in the French Renaissance château style (shades of Blois and Chenonceau but with Scottish overtones), the college succeeds as a spectacular piece of architecture on two levels; firstly, as a city silhouette, its jagged outine in marked contrast with the deciduous woodland around and, secondly, as a daring compilation of rich and varied details — aggressive gargoyles craning forth from the splendid towers, elegant wrought-iron work tripping along the roofline and elaborate scrollwork crawling back and forth across the main facade. Stone, slate and lead have weathered to an attractive homogeneous shade with lamp standards, lozenge glass and timber largely intact. Behind the main facade protrudes the magnificent chapel. Occasionally, foreign visitors to the city mistakenly assume the building to be the castle — an understandable mistake in view of its arresting appearance!

Café Royal, Edinburgh

1863

Café Royal, West Register Street, Edinburgh
Robert Paterson

Edinburgh's Café Royal can be found deep in the meanderings of West Register Street. Occupying an inconspicuous corner site, the building — the second to bear the name — was designed by a local architect, Robert Paterson. Since its opening on July 8th 1863, the 'New Café Royal Hotel' (as it was then styled) has undergone many changes, although the ground floor interiors still retain a fantastic opulence, epitomising as they do Victorian taste and flamboyance. Visitors to the building can still admire the wealth of fine stained glass created by the city firm of J Ballantyne and Co., the elaborate gilded plasterwork on ceilings and cornices, the intricate timber finishes, and a splendid series of ceramic murals installed by J McIntyre Hendry around 1925. While making the most of its cramped location, the exterior does not adequately suggest the decorative splendour achieved on the inside. This, then, makes for a pleasant surprise for those entering the Café for the first time.

1864

Barclay Church, Bruntsfield Place, Edinburgh
Frederick Thomas Pilkington

Pilkington is thought to have been much influenced by the writings and teachings of John Ruskin, who gave a series of talks in Edinburgh in 1853 making known his preference for a Northern Italian Gothic style. His publication *Stones of Venice* (1851-1853) highlighted the importance of an organic architecture which gave pleasure to the craftsmen involved in creating it, and the vigorous modelling of Pilkington's Barclay Church in Bruntsfield Place, coupled with the profusion of leaf-like ornament there, seems to embody this principle. The church is a Herculean affair; at ground level a seething mass of energetic elements colliding into each other as they vie for supremacy. Out of all this a particularly splendid banded masonry spire struggles free to rise majestically above the adjacent parkland. It is a substantial, sculpted building — awkward blocks of undressed stone protruding from plain walls and contrasting with the wealth of carved foliage creeping across the facade. Here is a church awesome in its enormity, all the elements of a great cathedral compressed together on a ridiculously small site. Little protrusions, finials and columns momentarily escape before being hauled back into this restless composition — even the roofs are complex and convoluted. Of such stuff bad dreams are made! But for all this, the spire is extremely elegant — tall, slim and in finely worked stone. To the left, on the entrance facade, is a grand rose window swathed in bands of polychromy. Pilkington designed churches in

Irvine, Penicuik, Innerleithen and Kelso, all with the same vibrant characteristics, although none as outstanding as this powerful building.

Barclay Church, Edinburgh

The Sliver Mill/Cox's Stack, Dundee

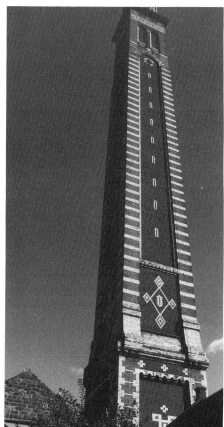

1865

The Sliver Mill/Cox's Stack, Dundee
George Cox/James MacLaren

Dundee had been long dependent on the growth of the textile industry when the introduction of jute — a coarse fibre imported largely from Bengal — signalled a significant increase in the construction of city mills and factories. This occurred during the 1850s and 60s, over which period mill engineers sought to improve the structural techniques involved, at the same time as generating building forms of some architectural merit. The Sliver Mill on Methven Street in Lochee, part of the huge Camperdown Works begun in 1861 by the engineer

The Sliver Mill/Cox's Stack, Dundee

George Cox, succeeded in satisfying both criteria — although not to the same extent as the remarkable Cox's Stack which towers alongside it. This soaring pinnacle of red and white brickwork, 280 feet high and in the style of an Italian campanile, is the finest surviving example of decorative chimneywork in Scotland. It was built in 1865 to the designs of Cox and James MacLaren, at a cost of £6,000. It is most impressive when seen in juxtaposition with the attractive cast-iron cupola of the mill and the elegant lamps which surmount the gateposts at the entrance to the complex.

1866

Hospitalfield House, Arbroath
Patrick Allan-Fraser

Hospitalfield House, Arbroath

Hospitalfield House derives its name from the former Hospitium of the Abbey of Arbroath, the medieval remains of which were incorporated into the present mansion during its construction. The Frasers of Hospitalfield became first associated with the estate during the middle of the seventeenth century, and Sir Walter Scott is known to have stayed there during the preparation of his novel *The Antiquary*. Hospitalfield was subsequently featured in the work under the guise of 'Monkbarns'. The building owes its present sprawling appearance to Patrick Allan, an artist of some prominence who married Elizabeth Fraser, heiress to the estate. The house comprises two substantial wings, at the intersection of which stands a corbelled, crow-stepped tower with views to the sea. The treatment of each wing is quite different, but with a distinctive crenellated cornice linking the two at parapet level. The shorter wing, which houses the drawing-room and picture gallery, was raised over the old stone walls of the original building — with a doorway dating back to 1325 neatly preserved as a seating niche. Above this, three shallow oriels bulge from the stonework, while the end facade features two huge turrets, sunk low and partially buttressed with a tall tri-partite window between. The interior is splendidly finished with a wealth of cedar panelling, and there is a particularly fine carved stone fireplace in the gallery. Shortly after completing work on the house, Allan-Fraser designed an exceptionally ornate Mortuary Chapel in Arbroath's Western Cemetery (1875).

1867

The Albert Institute, Albert Square, Dundee
Sir George Gilbert Scott

Albert, the Prince Consort, died in 1861. In recognition of his lifetime promotion of science and the arts, a group of Dundee citizens founded the Albert Institute Company Ltd., one of the directors of which was the Bishop of Brechin. Having successfully completed two churches for the Bishop, the first of which had been St. Paul's Cathedral in Dundee (1853), George Gilbert Scott was in a good position to secure the commission for the planned Institute. His appointment was confirmed in March 1864, and a central site known as 'The Meadows' purchased from the Town Council. This purchase was on the condition that the Institute — to be dedicated to science, literature and the arts — would have a free library on the premises. In order to overcome the treacherous nature of the marshy site, £10,000 worth of oak piles had to be sunk below ground level before work could begin. These were replaced in concrete in 1906. Scott reported that the building would incorporate "... a great hall ... (in) the best period of pointed architecture ... (with) such national characteristics as render it distinctly Scottish". Try as he might, however, Scott could not shake off the memories of his many European sketching trips and, as a result, the swirling elliptical staircase, the lead and timber flêche, the steep roofs, and even the gable crow-steps are a trifle Frenchified. The Albert Hall itself was opened in September 1867 and the reference and lending libraries in July 1869. Later, however, various additions were made to the rear and sides, and these considerably overelongate the original composition.

The Albert Institute, Dundee

1868

Bank of Scotland Headquarters, The Mound, Edinburgh
David Bryce

The full potential of the great precipitous north facade of Robert Reid and Richard Crichton's Bank of Scotland headquarters on the Mound (1806) remained unexploited until David Bryce was commissioned to alter and extend

Bank of Scotland Headquarters, The Mound, Edinburgh

the premises around 1865. Bryce responded to this not inconsiderable challenge by almost completely wrapping the original building in a cloak of Roman Baroque detailing, adding two lateral wings with 'campanile', and a rather bulbous dome whose silhouette was later altered slightly by Peddie and Kinnear. If Reid and Chrichton's scheme had been a 'prominent deformity', Bryce succeeded in erasing virtually all traces of it, leaving in its place an elaborate composition, highly embellished and vigorously articulated. The impressive north front gives way to a fine pavilioned terrace, rebuilt by Peddie and Kinnear in 1878. Below this fall the lush contours of the Princes Street Gardens, the foliage of which nicely softens the base of this monumental pile.

Great Western Terrace, Glasgow

1869

Great Western Terrace, Great Western Road, Glasgow
Alexander Thomson

Within the mile or so which separates the Botanical Gardens at the head of Byres Road, and the Gartnavel General Hospital, lies the finest stretch of Glasgow's Great Western Road. Lined on either side by magnificent terraces and villas, this long gracious avenue features the work of some of the city's most prominent Victorian architects. Of these many buildings, Alexander Thomson's Great Western Terrace is the best. Designed in 1867, it has the striking pavilions of Wilson's Kirklee Terrace (1846), the powerful rhythm of J T Rochead's Grosvenor Terrace (1855), and the simplicity of some of the lesser known tenements. It has an exceptional severity, however, enlivened only briefly by the delicate cast-iron railings and lamp standards. Elsewhere, there is a scarcity of detail — only the restrained use of Ionic porches and a decorative cornice at roof level. It depends largely for its success on the clever massing —

on the manner in which the pavilions appear not at the end of the terrace but further in, allowing the lower section to pass through to the end elevations where the building falls to a podium housing the handsome entrance steps and ramps. Given the superb examples carried out by his predecessors along this length of the thoroughfare, it might not have been enough for Thomson to have designed the building in his often exuberant fashion. Instead, he adopted a controlled simplicity, and far surpassed them all.

1870

'Coll-Earn', High Street, Auchterarder
William Leiper

'Coll-Earn', Auchterarder

Despite having been of a "shy and retiring disposition", William Leiper accumulated commissions with an enviable ease. A sizeable proportion of his domestic work is concentrated in the Helensburgh area, where few architects could better the French/Scottish-inspired baronial mansions he built there. 'Coll-Earn', just off Auchterarder's High Street, was the first country house Leiper designed in this 'Franco-Scotto' manner — an attractive, turreted red sandstone villa with buff dressings, sculptured panels, delightful bird and animal finials, crow-steps, tourelles and exceptionally decorative dormers. The interior, decorated by the stained glass artist Daniel Cottier, is furnished in the 'Anglo-Japanese' style (a movement in art supported by non-revivalists, but of which few intact examples have been unearthed in Scotland), with a wealth of painted tile panels, stained glass and simple timberwork. As is the case with the majority of Leiper's private houses, the tiny gate-lodge seated at the foot of the approach to 'Coll-Earn' is an endearing miniature of the parent building.

1871

The Egyptian Halls, 84–100 Union Street, Glasgow
Alexander Thomson

Thomson's style is unmistakable, whether the building in question be warehouse, terrace, villa or church. The Egyptian Halls in Glasgow could be by

The Egyptian Halls, Glasgow

no other — a logical progression in the architect's unique development of a warehouse design, a grid-like facade of robust and unusual character. In essence there is only a street elevation, a ceaseless and powerful rhythm of vertical divisions, something of a catalogue of columns in that the supports at each storey level are marked by a distinct and individual treatment. While these elements of the structure remain the same width as they rise through the building, they are tall pilasters with an advanced 'T' piece at first floor level, the reverse — coupled pilasters with a recessed panel between — on the second floor, and dwarf columns — little and fat and with Egyptianesque capitals — on the top storey. Above is a weighty and exceptionally ornate entablature. The third floor 'eaves' gallery exhibits the same daring characteristic as the ground floor bay window at 'Holmwood' (1858), with the columns quite free of the glazing behind. By comparison, the ground floor was relatively plain. The building, however, could do with a good scrub, lacking as it does the gaiety suggested by the wealth of beautiful ornament.

Bethelnie Steading, Meldrum

1872

Bethelnie Steading, Meldrum
James Duncan

In the union of agriculture and architecture, the latter is generally subservient to the other; form really is dictated by function. This is not to say, however, that Scotland's rural sheds, stables and steadings are without appeal, for they make a significant contribution to the initial impact of this country's landscape. At Bethelnie Steading in Meldrum — a grey granite building set against a bleak stretch of hills and at the end of a long, grass-fringed track — gablets, dormers and shallow arches have been used to lend rhythm and definition to the entrance facade. This main front comprises two bothies, single storey and with attics and each located at opposite ends of the building, a range of cart sheds in the centre, and two pends, which separate bothies and sheds and which are contained within advanced, gabled sections leading to the heart of the layout. All this is neatly expressed in a restful, symmetrical composition, the whole sheltering under a long, slated roof. Designed by James Duncan in 1872, Bethelnie Steading — diminutive and unaffected — both humanises and accentuates the expansive sprawl of land of which it is the focal point.

1873

The Kibble Palace, Botanic Gardens, Glasgow
John Kibble

A vast spreading filigree of glass and iron, rivalled in delicacy only by the ferns and foliage housed below, immediately envelops the visitor to Glasgow's Kibble Palace. Formerly styled the Kibble Crystal Art Palace, this elegant structure was first erected alongside the Coulport retreat of John Kibble, a gentleman whose talents extended to engineering, astronomy and photography. It is likely that he collaborated on the design of the conservatory with Boucher and Cousland, the architects of the house. In 1872, having negotiated the reconstruction of the glasshouse at the Royal Botanic Gardens in Glasgow, Kibble had it dismantled and towed upriver from Loch Long. During the reassembly, the main dome was enlarged and a substantial entrance foyer comprising a central corridor with two transepts and a small dome at the crossing was created. This airy space was filled with rock gardens, fountains, exotic plants and statues. Initially, Kibble had envisaged that he would have the use of the space for recitals, shows and exhibitions for twenty years, at the end of which time he would relinquish ownership of the property. In fact, the management of the Botanic Gardens purchased the remainder of the lease in 1881. Shortly after, the Glasgow Corporation assumed ownership of the Gardens, which accordingly became a public park. Today, with its magnificent collection of mosses and ferns, dazzling statues, ornamental fish pond and awesome swathe of barely supported glass above and around, the Kibble Palace is open to all, delicate and delightful.

The Kibble Palace, Glasgow

The Kibble Palace (interior)

Glasgow University, Glasgow

Glasgow University, Gilmorehill, Glasgow
Sir George Gilbert Scott

Glasgow is a city of hills, a good many of which are concentrated in the west end. Woodlands Hill, one of the most prominent, is graced with the lively Park Circus development (1855), while sited in a much more erect fashion on the opposite side of the River Kelvin are the Glasgow University buildings on Gilmorehill. The University, founded in 1451, vacated its High Street premises in 1870 in favour of its present accommodation. George Gilbert Scott was appointed to design the complex, and elected to work in "a style which I may call my own . . . already initiated . . . in the Albert Institute at Dundee . . . a thirteenth or fourteenth-century secular style with the addition of certain Scottish features . . .". Long and low, with an impressive central tower and twin quadrangles, the building was left unfinished by Scott, whose son John Oldrid completed the Bute Hall with its magnificent vaulted undercroft, and added the distinctive and delicate spire which so enhances the south facade. The selection of Scott to design these new premises was a source of much aggravation amongst local architects. Nonetheless, the commission was the largest in Britain since the building of the Houses of Parliament, and Scott — the most prolific of the Gothic Revivalists — proved that he was nothing if not equal to the task.

1875

McEwan Hall, Teviot Place, Edinburgh
Sir Robert Rowand Anderson

One can forgive Robert Rowand Anderson his over-energetic Italian exterior
for Edinburgh University's McEwan Hall once actually inside the building.
Here, a splendid ribbed dome, lavishly gilded and decorated on the underside,
hovers over a sweeping, spacious interior — close-centred columns supporting
two semi-circular gallery levels and, above these, a series of arches topped by
bug-eyed circular lights. It is an immensely grand auditorium, designed as part
of an extensive programme of additions to the University complex, a
programme which also made provision for the design of the Medical School in
Teviot Row. Located alongside the McEwan Hall, these 'New Buildings', as
they were named, exhibit a shade more restraint than their jolly neighbour, with
the bouncing, enthusiastic rhythm of the hall facade slowing to a more relaxed
pace in the coupled, arched windows of the Medical buildings.

McEwan Hall, Edinburgh

Chapel and Library, Dunecht House, Echt

1876

Chapel and Library, Dunecht House, Echt
George Edmund Street

Dunecht House began life as a neo-Greek villa subsequently absorbed by a larger Italianate composition. In 1864, Lord Alexander Lindsay, owner of the estate of Echt, resolved to enlarge the house by the addition of a library and chapel. Lindsay was passionately interested in Christian art and architecture, and had already determined that the extension would be in the 'Italico-Lombard style' long before appointing the architect George Edmund Street to prepare plans. Street was a prominent ecclesiologist who preferred to work in the Gothic style, but who nonetheless responded admirably to Lord Lindsay's request. And so, the library and chapel are Romanesque in appearance — the library top-lit and with blank arcaded walls. Centred on the west facade is an elaborate bay containing the reading room, which is flanked on either side by stair turrets with rising string courses and narrow windows. The sombre monumentality of this exterior gives way to a light and graceful interior, with much cast-iron, timber and polished granite. The chapel is tall and narrow, with a fine Lombardic entrance porch and elegant belfry. The combination of the main elements of the chapel and library — a chequered parapet at roof level, arches, niches and crow-steps — results in a strange, yet pleasing composition. There is also an attractive entrance tower to the rear, linking the original building to its stately extension.

91–117 Hope Street, Glasgow

1877

91–117 Hope Street, Glasgow
J Dick Peddie and Charles Kinnear

Never were seven storeys and three principal facades so crowded with windows, dormers, pilasters and chimneys as at Nos. 91–117 Hope Street in Glasgow's city centre. Begun as a hotel on ground acquired by the Caledonian Railway Company for their new Central Station, the architects — Peddie and Kinnear — proposed that the building would have "no lavish display of ornamentation". In fact, given the uniformity of painterwork and the control exercised over window replacements, the building — now shops and offices — is adequately decorative without the need for applied ornament, with a very powerful rhythm set up on the Hope Street facade which continues around both corners. *The British Architect* of July 1890 carried an illustration of the main facade, which then featured "an arcade, or open space in the centre of the building . . . covered in by an ornamental roof of iron and glass". Mention was also made of the use of elevators in the scheme, in addition to which there are several grand staircases leading to generous arched corridors. The change in use which occurred was initiated by the decision, in 1880, to convert what began as the offices of the Central Station into what is now the station hotel.

1878

Atholl Palace Hotel, Pitlochry
Andrew Heiton

Atholl Palace Hotel, Pitlochry

Perched jauntily on a gentle hillock and outlined against a broad band of trees, the former Atholl Hydropathic in Pitlochry creates an almost fairy-tale silhouette; two semi-circular towers topped by high, conical roofs (interrupted once by horizontal strips of glazing), little dormers, pyramidal roof forms and flagpoles galore. An enormous establishment, and now the Atholl Palace Hotel, it was designed by Andrew Heiton — Perth's City Architect from 1856 — and was built at a cost of £100,000. The two main aspects of the building are quite different — the north-west facade a 'U' shape with gabled centrepiece and entrance porch; the south-east elevation (that with the two turrets) having an elegant ground floor verandah with a semi-glazed winter garden feature over. The approach to the hotel passes tantalisingly close to this elaborate front before sweeping around the building to the rear and entrance.

1879

Mount Stuart, near Kerrycroy, Bute
Sir Robert Rowand Anderson

In completing the mansion of Mount Stuart on the Island of Bute in 1885, Robert Rowand Anderson became the architect responsible for "probably the most eclectic as well as the most sumptuous design for a late Victorian country

Mount Stuart, Bute

house in Scotland". Commissioned by the third Marquess of Bute to rebuild the house after the original had burnt down, Rowand Anderson set about creating a great medieval palace complete with chapel and tower. Begun in 1879, the main body of the house was built in a red sandstone with all manner of tracery and mouldings. Supported above the second floor were a further floor and attic, the former with an external gallery and walls of brickwork set in oak framing. An elegant stone balustrade carries the spreading eaves above, the roof sweeping up past little Flemish dormers to a ridge punctuated by tall chimney stacks. There are balconies, buttresses and bay windows; conservatories and cloisters; arches and pends — all designed to articulate the exterior and enliven the composition, the richness thus achieved rivalled only by the interior where there are lavish displays of marble, timber, stained glass, bronze and stencilled paintwork. Luckily, alterations to this grand house have been kept to a minimum.

Queen Street Station, Glasgow

#

Queen Street Station, North Hanover Street, Glasgow
James Carswell

The demolition in 1975 of Glasgow's St. Enoch Station left the city with a sole surviving vaulted railway station — Queen Street High Level. Since the disappearance of the original terminus buildings, the station has altered considerably, although the final approach to the high level platforms remains essentially the same. At Cowlairs commences the incline which marks the descent into the last half-mile tunnel. This gash in the rock is crowded on either side by looming multi-storey blocks and dilapidated factories. The track passes into the gloom of the tunnel — every sound amplified — and then, suddenly, the graceful spreading ceiling of the station roof illuminates the last few hundred yards. This great roof, whose light and airy characteristics are in such marked contrast to the approach, was erected under a series of improvements initiated by the North British Railway Company. In September 1878 a contract was signed with P and W McLellan of Glasgow to construct this new roof, the design provided by James Carswell, the railway company's chief engineer. When completed in 1880, the roof spanned 250 feet, curved to a maximum height of 75 feet and took the form of a splendid glazed arch, supported by double arched trusses with diagonal bracing and resting on Corinthian cast-iron columns. For some time a magnificent glazed, arched end welcomed visitors to the Queen Street entrance to the station. This, alas, is now hidden.

1881

Queen's Cross Church, Carden Place/Albyn Place, Aberdeen
John Bridgeford Pirie

The great granite edifices of Aberdeen have in common a lasting ability to retain the very precise nature of their architecture; details are seldom distorted and concepts rarely blurred by the passing of time. This is especially true of John B Pirie's largest and most successful piece of work — the Queen's Cross United Free Church of 1881, the competition brief for which had stipulated that "the buildings shall be of best Aberdeen or Kemnay granite . . .". Like many before him, Pirie was sufficiently impressed by the writings of John Ruskin to confine the bulk of his work to the Gothic style. As illustrated by the Queen's Cross Church, however, his use of the style carried with it a strong streak of individualism — the French Gothic of the stunningly elegant spire reworked with great flair and assurance. This splendid tower — square with tall lancet windows in its lower stages and octagonal thereafter, with an open colonnette supporting the stonework above — is a prominent feature of the city's west end. More unusual, however, is the church hall which exhibits the 'Proto-Secessionist' characteristics which Pirie developed in the design of a large number of unusual private houses in Aberdeen — the most original of which is a complex little villa at No. 50, Queen's Road (1885).

Queen's Cross Church, Aberdeen

1882

'The Bughties', 76 Camphill Road, Barnhill, Dundee
John Murray Robertson

The work of John Murray Robertson featured prominently in the architectural development of late Victorian Dundee. He practised first in a style similar to that of Alexander 'Greek' Thomson, and latterly in a Jacobean idiom. He was particularly interested in the design of contemporary American houses however, details of which had begun to appear in British architectural publications by the 1880s. 'The Bughties' in Barnhill, a suburb of Dundee,

'The Bughties', Dundee

illustrates well the extent of this influence — an attractive half-timbered mansion built for Colonel H B Fergusson, a jute manufacturer. The massing of the house is particularly picturesque — sited high above Camphill Road behind a screen of trees, and with distinctive red brick chimneys rising up from an array of gablets, hips and rosemary tiles. A stencilled frieze appears at sporadic intervals along the stone course beneath the projecting eaves, and there is a single storey, twin bay-windowed extension stretching out to the east. All this is built in a pale red sandstone with timber detailing currently highlighted in grey and white. Internally, there is much timber panelling and an unusual stair banister featuring a Japanese sun-flower motif.

The City Chambers, George Square, Glasgow
William Young

Pomp and exuberance are the hallmarks of Glasgow's City Chambers. Lavish both internally and out, resplendent in its Dunmore and Polmaise stone finish, it has an air of bourgeois self-esteem made all the more remarkable by the fact that construction began barely five years after the spectacular collapse of the City of Glasgow Bank. What the building lacks in finesse then, it more than makes up for in determination and vigour. William Young, a Paisley born architect who ran a London-based practice, won the competition held to secure a design for the scheme, and the foundation stone was duly laid on October 6th 1883. Construction took five years, with over ten million bricks sandwiched between the ornate stone cladding and the splendid finishes within. Polished granites, faience, veined marbles, hardwoods, freestone, mosaic — all these and

The City Chambers, Glasgow

more were used in the creation of a sumptuous and durable interior. Externally, the building boasts four extensive frontages wrapped around a central quadrangle, the whole dominated by a great square tower with an elaborate cupola, seen best towering over the principal entrance off George Square. If Glasgow had thought to better the town halls of Greenock and Paisley, both of which preceded the City Chambers, then the attempt was an impressive one.

Well Court, Edinburgh

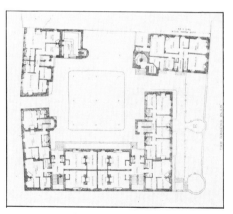

1884

Well Court, Dean Village, Edinburgh
Sydney Mitchell

Dean Village fits snugly into the valley of the Water of Leith, close to the western part of Edinburgh's New Town. While overlooked on all sides by the city, it retains a character and identity all of its own — the village, isolated by the dramatic topography of its location, developing around the meal mills which supplied Edinburgh. In 1884, a local philanthropist John R Findlay (owner of *The Scotsman*) determined to better the lot of the workers, and appointed Sydney Mitchell to design a model housing scheme on the north bank of the river. The scheme comprised two 'L'-shaped blocks of flats linked over an arched pend giving access to a courtyard and washing green. At the south-east corner of the site there was a social hall with an attractive ogival-roofed clock tower. Hall and housing were linked by a perimeter wall which dropped to the river's edge. Notwithstanding the smallness of some of the flats, there were a substantial number of internal toilets and separate sculleries. The grouping of the buildings, which is extremely picturesque, remains largely unchanged. The exterior, judiciously detailed in a seventeenth century Scots idiom, with handsome stair towers, steep slated roofs, dormers, crow-steps and projecting eaves, has retained the ability to enchant. Visible from Lindsay's house at Rothesay Terrace, the physical manifestation of his concept must have given him a great deal of enjoyment.

Place of Tilliefour, Aberdeenshire

1885

Place of Tilliefour, Aberdeenshire
Hew Montgomerie Wardrop

Tilliefour, situated in an especially remote part of Aberdeenshire, originally comprised a small rubble-built tower house dating back to the seventeenth century, and which lay in a ruinous condition for some time before being renovated and enlarged around 1885. The additions, designed by Hew Montgomerie Wardrop, seem extensive when compared to the original building, although their length is cleverly reduced through the fragmentation of the scheme into a series of gabled, crow-stepped and chimneyed blocks rather randomly clustered together in the manner of a group of little bothies. Thus, the scale and character of the tower house are not swamped by the more recent work. Robert Rowand Anderson, Wardrop's partner, succeeded to the commission on the death of the other man, immediately despatching north the young Robert Lorimer who, in his capacity as the site architect responsible for the supervision of the work, learned much that was to stand him in good stead in his future role as one of Scotland's most nationalistic architects.

Warehouses, James Watt Dock, Greenock

1886

Warehouses, James Watt Dock, East Hamilton Street, Greenock
William Kinipple

Greenock has not yet lost the drama associated with shipbuilding and industry. Docks remain lined with cranes, the approach from Glasgow still overlooked by great walls of brick and cast-iron. Of these huge structures, the finest is the range of warehouses sited on the south quay of the James Watt Dock. The dock itself was begun in 1881, amid much controversy over the choice of site, where it was felt that "the chances of paying for this dock by transatlantic traffic intercepted on the way to Glasgow are very shadowy". The warehouses, parallel to road and river, stretch for a total of 676 feet. Two blocks, five storeys high with attics, have highly decorative gables featuring blank arches, the forms of which are picked out in white brickwork against a background of red. The remaining two warehouses are low and with valley roofs, each gabled to the street and punctuated by a series of twin arches with brick and window infill and small, circular vents. This south elevation is hugely energetic, with a dizzying rhythm when viewed at speed. The quayside facade was built on a cast-iron beam and column system. Railway connections were made to the new dock, with lines passing through the warehouses which enabled wagons to be loaded at any point within the buildings. There, the ingenious provision of valve flaps in the columns allowed them to be used as chutes for transferring grain from one floor to another.

Warehouses, James Watt Dock, Greenock

1887

Central Library, George IV Bridge, Edinburgh
Sir George Washington Browne

The design of Edinburgh's principal public library was fraught with unusual problems for the architects who elected to compete for the commission in 1887. The peculiarities of the site demanded that the competitors successfully overcome the 48 foot drop from the George IV Bridge on the east, to the Cowgate below; furthermore, to the north was a high, rather shabby gable wall which required to be effectively disguised. To the winning architect, however, these contraints posed few difficulties; his solution was to locate the bulk of the library accommodation 10 feet behind the parapet of the bridge (thus permitting light to reach the lower levels) and to use the main staircase — brought forward onto the streetline — to achieve the necessary link with the adjacent building. Thus, from the main entrance — the only point at which bridge and building connect — the general reading room was down, and the reference room up; the latter originally "capable of accommodating 160 male readers and 36 female readers in the wing . . . set apart and screened off for the use of ladies". George Washington Browne designed the library in his favourite Francois ler style; the facade to the George IV Bridge lavishly detailed and topped by an enjoyable roofline. On the south and rear, where the treatment is more sombre, the building falls through three storeys to the level of the Cowgate.

Central Library, Edinburgh

Stirling High School, Spittal Street, Stirling

1888

Stirling High School Extension, Spittal Street, Stirling
James MacLaren

The Arts and Crafts Movement of the 1880s and 1890s marked a transitional
phase between the preceding period, which had been chiefly preoccupied with
historicism, and the years which followed with the birth of modern
architecture. Primarily an English phenomenon, Scottish architects whose
work was sympathetic to the ideals of the movement included John Bridgeford
Pirie in Aberdeen, William Gillespie Lamond in Dundee, and James MacLaren
of Stirling. In Glasgow, Charles Rennie Mackintosh and James Salmon
brought their individual applications of the Art Nouveau style to bear on the
development of Scottish architecture. MacLaren, in his search for a
"'vernacular' architecture in a modern adaptation" left Stirling for London
around 1877, although his first large-scale commission was for the addition of
an observatory tower and new wing to his former high school. The tower is
magnificent — remotely Baronial — with a great cliff of a wall abruptly
throwing out a circular turret whose ogival roof clearly anticipates
Mackintosh's *Glasgow Herald* Building of 1893. It is, however, looser than
Baronial, unprettified and with a massing in whose originality can be seen the
influence of the "free Romanesque" of the American architect H H Richardson.
A highly individual building, the extension met with favourable criticism in the
architectural press of the time, who saw "naturalistic" elements in its aggressive,
powerful stance.

1889

Templeton's Carpet Factory, Glasgow Green, Glasgow
William Leiper

A glorious brick and tile tapestry hung against the rapidly disappearing grime
of Glasgow's East End, William Leiper's extension to the Templeton's Carpet

Templeton's Carpet Factory, Glasgow

Templeton's Carpet Factory, Glasgow

Factory gave the city a unique facade, a building of "permanent architectural interest and beauty". James Templeton and Son had first established their carpet weaving business on the site at Glasgow Green in 1857, later commissioning Leiper to design the facade to their extension for the manufacture of spool Axminster carpets. The architect was no mean colourist, his domestic work usually characterised by a wealth of stained glass and stencilwork, and although the scheme bears a passing similarity to the Doge's Palace in Venice, it is by no means a slavish copy — more a colourful, witty comment on the firm's products. The bulk of the elevation, begun in 1888, is constructed from a rich red terracotta brick, with stone dressings, spandrel panels of blue mosaic, glazed brick and faience. There is a modicum of carving and sculpture, but the building relies for effect on the initial impact created by the brilliance of colour and the rhythm of arch piled upon arch. Happily, Leiper's theme was continued in the adjacent extension, and from the south of the park a frieze of pattern and colour can be seen dancing above a border of trees.

1890

Fortingall Hotel and Kirkton Cottages, Fortingall
Dunn and Watson/James MacLaren

MacLaren died when only forty-seven, and his practice was inherited by the partnership of William Dunn and Robert Watson. He had spent the final years of his life in the design of a series of buildings in Perthshire, the majority of which represented commissions from Sir Donald Currie of Garth, who was anxious to remodel the estate around Glenlyon House in Fortingall. The improvements thus initiated included an attractive range of thatched cottages built to house farm workers from the estate. The tradition of reed thatching had been long abandoned in the area before this time; nevertheless, reeds harvested from the Tay estuary at Errol were brought to the site to provide a distinctive roof finish. The scheme was enlarged in 1913 through the addition of a further four cottages which, while faithful to the spirit of the original, were built on a larger scale and without the interesting array of planes which occurs at the corner of MacLaren's composition. Shortly after his death, Dunn and Watson rebuilt Glenlyon House itself and designed the Fortingall Hotel. The essence of this building lies in its visual simplicity and permanence, in its

Fortingall Hotel, Fortingall

Kirkton Cottages, Fortingall

uncluttered appearance achieved through the use of harling, slating, gables, crow-steps, chimneys and dormers — all in a solid Scottish tradition. It is a low-key building, dozy even, but for the curious inclusion of two huge dressed stone piers on either side of the entrance. Between these spans a mammoth stone lintel on which is carved the title of the hotel, in lettering which hints at the style which became so characteristic of Charles Rennie Mackintosh. Dunn and Watson may not have had the same degree of flair that MacLaren showed, but the subtle incorporation of the second 'L' in 'Fortingall' as the upright of the preceding letter 'A' shows some cunning at least.

Charing Cross Mansions, Glasgow

1891

Charing Cross Mansions, Sauchiehall Street, Glasgow
Sir John James Burnet

During the early 1970s a great inner city ring road carved its way through and around the nucleus of Glasgow's west end. Charing Cross, where Sauchiehall Street met and passed St. George's Road, retained few of its original characteristics — an area devastated but for the proud sweep of the still extant Charing Cross Mansions. This haughty range of red sandstone tenements withstood the wrath of progress to have the grime of years spectacularly cleansed away and the clock and its attendant sculpture gilded and restored to working order. Completed in 1891, the Mansions have a restless air about them — accelerating rapidly around the corner in a flurry of bay windows, balconies, chimneys and cupola, before slowing to a gradual halt at the circular tower which marks the entrance to Renfrew Street. The architect, J J Burnet of Burnet, Son and Campbell, had spent some time studying at the Ecole des Beaux Arts in Paris when young, which may account for the French flavour which permeates the design. Closer to home, however, is Charles Wilson's Park Terrace (1855) from which the mansard roofs and dormers may have originated. Whatever this prolific young architect's sources of inspiration were, he succeeded in creating an effect both rich and sculptural — a constant source of fascination to the passerby, and a spectacular sight when glimpsed briefly from the motorway which passes beneath.

1892

The Athenaeum Theatre, 179 Buchanan Street, Glasgow
Sir John James Burnet with John A Campbell

During the 1890s, Glasgow began to expand in an upward direction, with slender Victorian buildings replacing the Georgian town houses which were being demolished in favour of higher, more commercially biased developments. The Athenaeum Theatre in Buchanan Street, built as an extension to the Glasgow Athenaeum College during this period, is typical of the trend — a deep, narrow building housing a theatre, dining rooms, music rooms and a gymnasium, with a lift and elliptical staircase located immediately behind the entrance facade. This elevation comprises, in effect, two dissimilar towers sited side by side in an unusual asymmetrical composition. One section — the wider — features a huge semi-circular headed indent, bridged at third floor level by a hefty stone bay window. This bulges out over more delicate bays below, with the outline of the indent repeated at roof level, where there is a grand sculpture niche with split pediment. By far the most interesting aspect of the building, however, is the right-hand part of the facade. Here, the rise of the staircase behind is followed by the rise of tall slit windows set between powerful stone mullions. It is these mullions, with their strong vertical emphasis, which allow one to imagine that the single, pedimented window at high level might slide up and down the rails on the facade, just as the lift inside moves up and down within its cage. Burnet and Campbell, from whose collaboration the building resulted, parted company in 1897 — although the latter pursued the theme of vertical emphasis in his subsequent buildings, of which the Northern Assurance Building of 1909 was one.

Ramsay Garden, Edinburgh

1893

Ramsay Garden, Castlehill, Edinburgh
S Henbest Capper

At the head of the picturesque line of buildings tumbling down the slope from the Castle Esplanade to West Princes Street Gardens in Edinburgh, sits a striking five storey block of flats — commissioned, conceived and financed in part by Sir Patrick Geddes, the noted botanist, town-planner and thinker. Forming an extension to Ramsay Lodge (incorporated at the heart of which is the curious octagonal house built for the poet Allan Ramsay in 1746), Ramsay Garden was intended to encourage men of professional standing to return to what was then an unfashionable part of the city in which to live. Geddes and his family immediately installed themselves in the twelve-roomed third floor of the "seven-towered castle" on its completion in 1893. Designed by S Henbest Capper, and operated initially on a co-operative basis, Ramsay Garden forms part of a folksy, attractive collection of buildings which is immediately evocative of the varied and distinctive architecture lining the Royal Mile.

1894

1–11 George Street, Doune
Thomas MacLaren

Thomas MacLaren, the designer of Nos. 1–11 George Street in Doune, was the brother of James Marjoribanks MacLaren, an architect of not inconsiderable talent who designed the Spittal Street extension to the Stirling High School

ATHENÆUM
GLASGOW

The Athenaeum Theatre, Glasgow

1–11 George Street, Doune

(1888). James, who died in 1890, is likely to have been a major influence on his brother, and several of the traditional Scottish features which the elder MacLaren favoured in his later work are in evidence in the Doune housing. Certainly the vocabulary of this stretch of George Street recalls sixteenth century Scottish detailing, with harled stonework, sandstone dressings, corbels and crow-stepped skews. The massing is picturesque, too, with one turret used to enhance the break in level of the roofs on either side, and another creating a visual stop between the housing itself and the adjacent property. Chimneys and dormers are neat, windows have small, square panes and the whole effect is very dainty. Not long after the completion of the scheme in 1894, MacLaren emigrated to America where he is known to have become a neo-classical designer.

1895

Jenners' Store, 47–52 Princes Street, Edinburgh
William Hamilton Beattie

Unscathed by the abrupt transformation of Princes Street during the 1950s and 60s, Jenners' store — the shadow of the Scott Monument (1840) flitting across its Baroque facade — is splendid advertising material. Stylish, swaggering and just a little bit strident, it gives the illusion of layer upon layer of rich icing on a cake into which one is sorely tempted to dig. It is late Victorian in the extreme, built during a period when Scotland was experiencing the first flushes of the Art Nouveau style. Hence, it is something of a maverick composition (seen in the context in which it has been placed here), but technically quite advanced, being

Jenners' Store, Edinburgh

fireproof and with an iron and steel frame and granolithic floors. While it is not altogether original (shades of Oxford's Bodleian Library (1613–36) in the plethora of paired columns) it negotiates the corner with considerable ease, topped by a jolly, stocky tower packed with frivolous ornament. Inside, there is an enjoyable mock Jacobean central well.

1896

Gardner Memorial Church, St. Ninian's Square, Brechin
Sir John James Burnet

Commencing with the development of the prototype at Shiskine on Arran in 1887, Burnet — over a period of about twenty years — designed a family of long, low, friendly churches, of which the Gardner Memorial Church at Brechin is one of the most attractive. Built in grey sandstone with red stone highlights, those features which are common to the series and which appear on the Brechin building include the square, squat tower capped with a pyramidal roof, the combination of Gothic and Romanesque detailing, and the long, cloister-like hall block. This church, however, is marked by some exceptionally fine sculpture and a smattering of wrought ironwork in which can be detected the influence of the Art Nouveau style. The interior is especially good, the cloister with a roof supported off handsome timber radial struts which spring up from stone corbels. Other churches of this ilk include the Broomhill Trinity Congregational Church in Glasgow (1900–08) and the MacLaren Memorial Church at Stenhousemuir (1897–1907).

Gardner Memorial Church, Brechin

Glasgow School of Art, Glasgow

1897

Glasgow School of Art, 167 Renfrew Street, Glasgow
Charles Rennie Mackintosh

The career of Charles Rennie Mackintosh has been well documented. His surviving works — which do not number many — have been much fêted, much photographed and expertly analysed — none more so than the Glasgow School of Art in Renfrew Street. Located on a narrow, steeply sloping site, the building was constructed in two phases and designed while Mackintosh was with the firm of Honeyman and Keppie. His is one of the few names linked with the brief appearance of the Art Nouveau style in Scotland — a European movement whose principal concern was with an architecture in two dimensions, ie the relationship between surface and ornament, the latter usually sinuous and exotic. Clearly, however, there is more to the School of Art than the gentle carving around the entrance, the distinctive wrought ironwork and the curvilinear treatment of the stonework. In fact, to categorise this building narrowly is to do it a sizeable injustice, since there are a number of influences in evidence — all endowed with Mackintosh's unique, slightly mystical, yet immensely practical touch. Through the design of this building, and others conceived in much the same spirit, Mackintosh secured for himself a prominent place in the history of the development of Scottish architecture.

1898

Melsetter House, Hoy, Orkney
William R Lethaby

Lethaby figured importantly in the development of the Arts and Crafts movement in England, although his favourite commission was located north of the border — Melsetter House on the Island of Hoy in Orkney. White harled and corbie-stepped, simple, but with some curious and creative decorative detailing, the mansion — built for Thomas Middlemore, a Birmingham businessman — perfectly embodies the design principles Lethaby and his colleagues endorsed, with — most importantly — a sense of rightness about the building. Essentially a plain, large-windowed composition with red sandstone trimmings, the house exhibits some wonderfully quaint features, such as the triple-gabled section at eaves level on the east facade, in the arrangement of which two downpipes play an unusually important role. There are also two dainty heart-shaped motifs on the adjacent gable. The house was requisitioned during both World Wars for use as naval quarters.

Melsetter House, Orkney

1899

St. Vincent Chambers, 142a–144 St. Vincent Street, Glasgow
James Salmon jnr.

Two gawping gargoyles (and none less friendly in the whole of Glasgow) loom over the main entrances to the incredible St. Vincent Chambers. Ten storeys high and with a frontage of barely 29 feet 6 inches in width, the building projects an almost ghoulish air, created largely through the extent to which stonework, balconies and dormers bulge, stretch and contort. All these convulsions, however, while tinged with the exoticism of the Art Nouveau idiom, were a means to a purely practical end; while the site was exceptionally narrow, it was also over 100 feet deep, and even with the inclusion of two

St. Vincent Chambers, Glasgow

lightwells incorporated close to the centre of the building, maximum glazing was required to light the interior. Not surprisingly, then, the most predominant feature of the main facade is glass, framed — for the most part — within twin oriel windows, piled one above the other on either side of central bipartite openings. At the very top, three lead-winged dormers sail out of an octagonal tower while, far below, on the underside of the oriels, is a wealth of flowing ornament. Structurally, it was rather daring, with the upper storeys cantilevered in steel off a double row of centrally located 'H' columns. Designed around 1898 by James Salmon jnr. of Salmon Son and Gillespie, the building has undergone a significant alteration since its completion — an elaborate finial which protruded from the tower, and which earned the property the nickname of 'The Hatrack', has been lopped off, thereby stunting the sinuous growth of this elegant little building.

1900

Marischal College, Aberdeen
A Marshall MacKenzie

Milan Cathedral came to Aberdeen at the turn of the century when Alexander Marshall MacKenzie adopted the same soaring, surging verticals to punctuate the Broad Street facade of Marischal College. The cold grey granite peculiar to the area suits well the crisp lines and many pinnacles — the darker horizontal joints combining with ribs and buttresses to create a dizzying, chequered effect. MacKenzie, while sympathetic to the revival of a Scottish 'vernacular', clearly thought this 'stately pile' better suited to the occasion. The existing complex — designed by Archibald Simpson in 1837 — was deemed to be sorely in need of enlargement by about 1891. In order to purchase and demolish the ancient buildings lining Broad Street, and rebuild the Greyfriars Church on the south-east corner of the quadrangle, the sum of £40,000 was cajoled from the Government. This allowed tenders to be let for the front block in May 1903. In the meantime, Simpson's central tower had been raised and the north-west wing extended. On completion of the Broad Street building, seven coats-of-arms were located above the huge archway, creating a splash of colour on an otherwise haughty, cool facade.

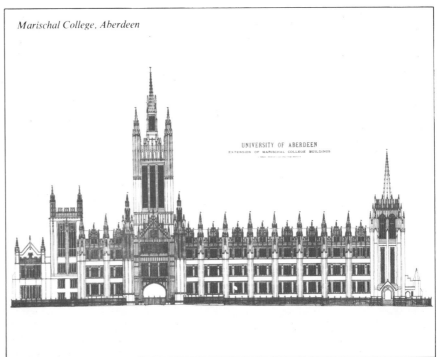

Marischal College, Aberdeen

UNIVERSITY OF ABERDEEN
EXTENSION OF MARISCHAL COLLEGE BUILDINGS

'Grey Walls', Gullane

1901

'Grey Walls', Gullane
Sir Edwin Landseer Lutyens

Lutyens dominated the English architectural scene over the first few decades of
the twentieth century. His was not a 'modern' architecture — this he had in
common with Robert Lorimer — but one based on a perpetual fascination with
traditional methods and materials. A major influence on the young Lutyens ·
was Richard Norman Shaw, a London Scot who was the ablest exponent of the
Arts and Crafts movement during the late nineteenth century. The approach to
the country house known as 'Grey Walls' in Gullane was much modified after
Lutyens had seen the curved screen wall at Chesters in Northumberland (1890)
by Shaw. The importance of 'Grey Walls' lies not so much in the house itself as
in the relationship between house and garden; the geometric disposition of
gates, walls and minor buildings upon the site. Access to the main driveway is
had from a primary courtyard at the end of which are three small lodges.
Between these are located two identical gateways, only one of which leads to
the house. The main approach route sets off on the diagonal, passing walled
gardens and outhouses before slowing up in the welcoming curve of the
symmetrical entrance facade. The facade is a falsehood, however, since behind
it the house breaks up in a most unsymmetrical fashion; the living quarters
contained within an 'H'-shaped block to the east. Rubble walled and roofed in
grey Dutch pantiles, 'Grey Walls' represents Lutyens' only sizeable
contribution to the Scottish landscape.

1902

'Wayside', 96 Hepburn Gardens, St. Andrews
Sir Robert Lorimer

Lutyens and Lorimer were friends for over twenty years, both impressed by the
other's work but neither finding much in common with Charles Rennie
Mackintosh, who was a contemporary. All three, however, were committed to
an architecture in which was incorporated the design of furniture, fittings and
finishes. Lorimer's early work owed much to the tenets of the Arts and Crafts
movement, although by the turn of the century both the impact of the
movement and his preoccupation with it were in decline. Around this time,

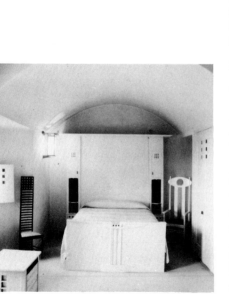

'Wayside', St. Andrews

however, he completed a series of whitewashed cottages near Edinburgh, in whose powerful roof forms and unusual dormer windows can be found the prototype of a stone built villa in St. Andrews. While the entrance elevation of 'Wayside' is relatively formal, both plan and south facade are fairly loosely arranged — the many different components of the latter knitted together under vast sweeping planes of slate. There is an impressive range of window shapes and sizes, from the two-storey high curved glazing wrapped around the hall, the horizontal opening set in a cusped dormer popping up amid a sea of slate, the oval featured in the patio wall, and the pair of openings set on either side of a tall, protruding chimney. Thus, roof and windows — the former hipped, curved, spreading and swelling — spectacularly reduce the scale of what is an extremely large house, each room or space highlighted in an individual manner. In this respect, the informality of 'Wayside' has more in common with Mackintosh's Hill House (1903) than appearances might at first suggest.

1903

Hill House, Upper Colquhoun Street, Helensburgh
Charles Rennie Mackintosh

Hill House, Bedroom

The Hill House in Helensburgh is splendidly situated to overlook the town below, the Clyde beyond and the hills of Renfrewshire on the horizon. Conversely, the house is not readily apparent until the distinctive wrought-iron entrance gates are reached, from where the full impact of this unique essay in domestic architecture can be appreciated. Built between 1902 and 1904 for the publisher W W Blackie, the austere, grey harled exterior — an amalgam of indigenous Scottish details highlighted by the occasional inclusion of an overtly modern feature — seems rather severe, sited as it is in an area where the exotic architecture of William Leiper predominates. Hill House, however, gains in subtlety through the omission of externally applied ornament. Instead, decorative detail (and ample of that) is confined to the interior, where furniture, fittings and finishes have all been afforded the same degree of attention as that paid to the studied informality of the external mass. Each room, and none more beautiful than the soothing pink and white master bedroom, unfolds as a set-piece for delicate stencilwork, glass and mosaic inlays, elegant light fittings, carpets, curtains — even clocks. In the design of Hill House, Mackintosh made reference to his previous scheme for 'Windyhill' at Kilmacolm (1901), and to his competition entry for "Das Haus eines Kunstfreundes" (House for an Art Lover). Sadly, his subsequent domestic commissions were of an insufficient scale to afford him the opportunity of developing further the themes of these fine houses.

Hill House, Helensburgh

Hill House, Helensburgh

1904

Scotland Street School, Glasgow

Charles Rennie Mackintosh

Scotland Street School, Glasgow

The clearance of Kingston during the 1970s gradually rendered Mackintosh's Scotland Street School obsolete, as the housing stock was drastically reduced to make way for the Glasgow Inner Ring Road. Mercifully, the school is to be retained as a Museum of Education — its grand glazed facade preserved for posterity; not as well known, nor as widely acclaimed as the School of Art, but a remarkable achievement nonetheless. Given the financial restraints by which Mackintosh must have been hampered, he has made considerable capital out of the situation — adopting a fairly standard school board plan which incorporates two separate entrances, two staircases and two sets of cloakrooms, but electing to express these in a most unusual fashion — the staircases as huge Scots-Baronial turrets, copiously glazed and with a modicum of decoration, and the cloakrooms stepping back the better to accentuate these powerful towers. With this curious, cloakroom cascade of stone and glass — each floor receding that little bit further than that below — Mackintosh saluted the arrival of the twentieth century and the coming of modernism.

1905

Wemyss Bay Station, Wemyss Bay

James Miller

Externally, Wemyss Bay Station gives nothing away. It is a playful, picturesque building — slightly curving, half-timbered and harled, and with a square, somewhat curious clock tower. The facade develops timbered sides and a glazed roof before finally pursuing a gentle slope down to the station pier, from where steamers ply back and forth across the Clyde. All is normal on the outside. Once inside, however, the effect becomes breathtaking. From a circular, stone built booking-office radiates a great glazed umbrella of a roof —

steel ribs springing to and fro between slim columns, the glazing encasing the central space before swirling off to follow the curve of the platforms in the one direction, and the concourse to the pier in the other. Here is a space of great drama, the very existence of which is belied by the unassuming exterior. Designed for the Caledonian Railway Company, the architect of the station was James Miller, whose flair for the exotic had already found form in the incredible Botanic Gardens Station, constructed for the same company in Glasgow but, sadly, destroyed by fire in 1970.

Wemyss Bay Station, Wemyss Bay

The Lion Chambers, Glasgow

1906

The Lion Chambers, 172 Hope Street, Glasgow
James Salmon jnr. and J Gaff Gillespie

Salmon and Gillespie were amongst the first architects in Scotland to exploit the structural and aesthetic possibilities of reinforced concrete. Faced with the daunting task of providing seemingly spacious office accommodation on a site barely wider than that of the St. Vincent Chambers (1899), and less than half as deep, they reduced the skin of the building to an incredible four inches thick by adopting the Hennebique system of construction, detailed in consultation with the structural engineer Louis-Gustave Mouchel. Using reinforced concrete columns, beams, walls and floor slabs, the Lion Chambers were raised eight floors above basement level and externally rendered in cement mortar. What little decoration there is on the west front was created 'in-situ' by using plaster moulds interwoven with steel. In order to complete external work, flying scaffolds were cantilevered out as each floor was finished, since the restrictions on the use of the site at street level prohibited the erection of a traditional scaffold. While the building lacks the sinuous appeal of the St. Vincent Chambers, it is as historically important — if not more so — in its imaginative use of a new material; the smooth finish and undulating north facade cleverly anticipating the stylistic trends of the Modern Movement. It is not yet stripped bare of the foibles of the Edwardian era, however, but comes daringly close for such a prominently located building.

1907

Stobswell School, Eliza Street, Dundee
William Gillespie Lamond

Stobswell School, Dundee

Lamond's first major commission was won while he was practising on his own account in Arbroath. There he built the looming, rumbustious Water Tower on Keptie Hill (1884) — executed in a brash Scots-Baronial style. The building shared with its architect an indomitable confidence — an attribute which

Lamond took with him when he left for Dundee around 1896. There, in 1907 and while with James H Langlands, he was given the opportunity of designing Stobswell School. In this building there is a concentration of detail around the main entrances, located on the short facade and sheltering beneath huge overhanging canopies. Much is made on this elevation of recessing the building twice on either side of the gabled centrepiece in order to disguise its considerable width. Thus, there is scope for two flanking towers with small cupolas, a small, curved ancillary room alongside each of these, and cloakrooms beyond. All this is constructed in a hammer-dressed rubble with smooth faced trimmings; infinitely less daunting than the shimmering elegance of Mackintosh's Scotland Street School (1904), but no less original. Great issue is made of the fenestration on this school — horizontal bands to the cloakrooms, huge arched openings to the library, and small, circular lights at the heads of the towers. Lamond proceeded to follow up this scheme with designs for the Dens Road Public School (1909) and the Eastern School at Broughty Ferry (1911), both testament to the fact that the exciting development of a Scottish Edwardian architecture was not confined to the west coast.

1908

St. Matthew's Church of Scotland, Gordon Street, Paisley
William McLennan

McLennan was a somewhat unorthodox designer who lived and worked in Paisley, was a contemporary of Mackintosh, and whose talent and powers of imagination — while occasionally close to those of the Glasgow architect — remain largely unacknowledged. His design for the St. Matthew's Church in Paisley, however, is an outstanding example of church architecture conceived in the Art Nouveau idiom. The building, as first envisaged, incorporated a huge, voluptuous tower where now sits a diminutive entrance; a vast, curiously out-of-scale effort which was startlingly original (and would have represented a major structural triumph) but which would have dominated the body of the church, obscuring some of its more subtle features. Of the elements which combine to make this such a delightful building, the most unusual are the graceful, curving corners of the nave mass. These appear in three separate guises in what is a rather wilfully asymmetric composition — the Gordon Street elevation, which includes some fine wrought-iron railings — presenting by far the best aspect. Windows are wide and patterned with an unusual tracery, and there are buttresses aplenty — some topped with odd, square battlements. Sited close to the town's Orchard Square, this church is superbly placed to be admired from all angles.

St. Matthew's Church of Scotland, Paisley

1909

Northern Assurance Building, 84–94 St. Vincent Street, Glasgow (rear facade)
John A Campbell

There is much of interest to see in Glasgow for those who are prepared to negotiate the narrow, dark lanes of the city centre. Mackintosh's remarkable *Daily Record* building (1901) lurks largely unnoticed in an alley, and J A Campbell's elegant rear facade to the Northern Assurance building is similarly hidden behind St. Vincent Street. Notwithstanding the three vertically surging bays of the main frontage, the public face of the building is a fairly conventional expression of the masonry loadbearing technique adopted above ground floor level. The rear, on the other hand, skilfully clothed in glazed brick and with large, metal casement windows, visibly capitalises upon the wide

Northern Assurance Building, Glasgow

spacing of the steel frame behind. In its visual honesty, this elevation heralded a move towards the crisp, no-nonsense articulation of many buildings of the 1930s and after, when facades of a similar nature were deemed quite suitable for use on front *and* rear.

First Church of Christ Scientist, Edinburgh

1910

First Church of Christ Scientist, Inverleith Terrace, Edinburgh
Ramsay Traquair

Few church architects had sites as spacious and attractive on which to build as that made available to Ramsay Traquair for the erection of the First Church of Christ Scientist on Inverleith Terrace. On either side of the broad, pleasant church are terraced gardens which fall away to the Water of Leith beyond. Thus, while the main body of the church is at street level, there is a generous, well lit hall beneath. Traquair, a pupil of Lorimer, detailed the building in a simple round-arched Scots Gothic style, with a wide transverse saddleback tower occupying the full breadth of the north facade, with nicely proportioned apsidal stair turrets on either gable. The simple, barrel-vaulted interior is brightly lit by five semi-circular headed windows on either side of the nave. These are set within squared recesses. The detail, from the flush triangulated arcades in dressed stone set high on the rubble-built stair towers, to the paucity of the tracery on the nave windows, suggests modesty and understatement. There is, however, a bold north cornice with a Celtic cross in relief centred on the parapet above.

Our Lady of The Assumption and St. Meddan's RC Church, Troon

1911

Our Lady of The Assumption and St. Meddan's RC Church, St. Meddan's Street, Troon
Dr Reginald Fairlie

The death, in 1900, of John Patrick Chrichton-Stuart, the third Marquess of Bute, robbed Scotland of one of its foremost architectural patrons of the period. Under his auspices the Bute Hall had been gifted to Glasgow University in 1877, and Mount Stuart on Bute spectacularly rebuilt in 1879. His will, however, gifted a sum of money to the Roman Catholic community in Troon — by which means they were able to erect the Church of Our Lady of the

Assumption and St. Meddan. Designed by Reginald Fairlie, who — like Traquair — had trained with Lorimer, the church was completed in 1911, a short, stocky building with a powerful stance — broad-shouldered and immutable. Fairlie favoured late fifteenth century Scottish church architecture, although the Troon building features round-headed as well as pointed windows. The detailing was derived, in part, from the Church of the Holy Rude in Stirling (c 1555); thus, there are crow-steps on the chancel roof, squat little buttress finials, and various splays on the buttresses themselves. Finally, just as the solidity of the church seems to become a little overpowering, up pops an endearing little timber spire, delicate and much crocketed, sitting pertly atop the staircase adjacent to the west tower.

1912

Formakin, Bishopton, Renfrewshire
Sir Robert Lorimer

The fact that the house of Formakin in Renfrewshire has remained unoccupied since its partial completion in 1914 should not be allowed to belittle the architectural achievement it represents. It was built to house the extensive tapestry collection of a stockbroker and art collector, John Holms, who appointed his architect friend Robert Lorimer to plan the development of the estate. Much influenced by the landscape work in England of Gertrude Jekyll (who frequently collaborated with Lutyens) Lorimer had the grounds planted first, giving them time to mature before work on the house began. Thus, the walled garden to the north of an existing farmhouse on the site was replanted as a pleasance, a formal walled garden extended to the east of this, and a vegetable garden created even further north. Construction of the house proper began in 1910, having been preceded by the completion of the distinctive ogee-roofed gate houses. Work on the red sandstone mansion was halted by the war however, the house unplastered internally but quite wind and watertight. In this condition it has since remained. Lorimer had determined that Formakin be "the purest Scotch I've ever done", and the result is a wholly traditional piece

Formakin, Renfrewshire

of work from an architect whose delight in simple craftsmanship enabled him to succeed in such ventures where others missed. In the meantime, the only permanent occupants of this abandoned masterpiece are the little stone monkeys caught clambering around the gatehouses and entrance posts.

Sandford House, Fife

1913

Sandford House, near Wormit, Fife
M Hugh Baillie-Scott

Had fire not stripped the thatched roof from Sandford Cottage near Wormit in September 1912, M H Baillie-Scott might not have been given the opportunity to transform the brick-clad holiday retreat he had designed ten years earlier for Harben J Valentine. The most significant feature of the first design had been the open-plan layout of the ground floor, where dining-room and parlour could be separated by movable screens. This relatively innovative planning characteristic was further developed by Baillie-Scott in his scheme for a series of twinned cottages for the Letchworth Garden City in Hertfordshire (1905), where the Voyseyesque combination of twin gables and sweeping roof planes on the main facade formed the basis of the enlarged south-east elevation to Sandford House. Baillie-Scott had, in fact, been requested by Valentine to extend the building before the fire occurred, but major alterations were initiated only after the house had been gutted. A wing containing outhouses and additional bedrooms was added to the north, while a double-height, partially sunken drawing-room with a huge expanse of window was built to overlook the Japanese garden created on the southern slope of the site by Valentine himself. This dramatic elevation, red-tiled and white-harled, rises steeply above the approach to what is now the Sandford Hill Hotel.

1914

North British Diesel Engine Works, 739 South Street, Glasgow
John Galt

Glasgow's industrial expansion during the years preceding the First World War was founded largely on shipbuilding and marine engineering, with the Clyde-based firm of Barclay Curle and Company the oldest and ablest in the city.

North British Diesel Engine Works, Glasgow

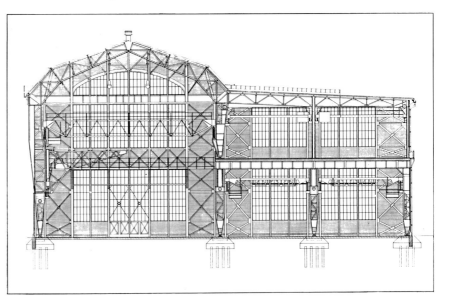

Architecture and industry were successfully combined in the building on which the firm collaborated with the North British Diesel Engine Company at Whiteinch. Built between 1913 and 1914, the machine hall, in which were housed huge moving gantries, was a large, steel-framed structure clad in brick and glass, linked to which was a two storey side hall, similarly constructed and with an almost flat roof. Structurally impressive within, the portal frame of the main space was translated externally as a long, low multi-faceted roof over a brick 'arch' infilled with glass. Unfortunately, the careful asymmetry of the complex has been upset by an extension to the west, and the whole building reclad in a material quite alien to the original aesthetic. While it is generally acknowledged that John Galt — a Glasgow architect — supervised the erection of the factory, recent research has suggested that the designer was a German engineer, Karl Bernhard, who worked with Peter Behrens on the design of the AEG Turbine Factory (1909) in Berlin — which would account for the clear similarities between the two buildings.

1915

Weir's Administration Building, Glasgow

Weir's Administration Building, 147 Newlands Road, Cathcart, Glasgow
Albert Kahn

Albert Kahn was a talented American architect who established a huge practice which specialised in the speedy design and economical erection of steel and reinforced concrete industrialised buildings. His early designs in concrete were commissioned by the Packard Automobile Company in Detroit, for whom he built a factory in 1905 on a still relatively experimental system. It was to this centre of America's burgeoning automobile industry that William Weir, of the Glasgow firm of engineers G and J Weir, came on one of his frequent business trips to the United States. Fascinated by motor cars, he was drawn to the Packard factories, and purchased plans for a building designed by Kahn and had his own workforce in Cathcart erect the scheme for use as an administration building. While not the first reinforced concrete structure in the city, the Weir's building still constituted a fairly early example — originally four storeys high and ten bays long by two (extremely wide) bays deep. Windows were large and steel framed, and the external face of the building was clad in concrete panels five inches thick, set between slightly protruding columns. The entrance, located to the east of the block, was highlighted by a red sandstone surround. So pleased was Weir by the results that he had an additional building — immediately used on completion as a munitions factory — built in the nearby Inverlair Avenue.

1916

East Suffolk Road Halls of Residence, Edinburgh

East Suffolk Road Halls of Residence, Edinburgh
Alan K Robertson

Robertson designed the East Suffolk Road Halls of Residence for the Moray House Training College in 1914, although he was unable to see the project through to site completion, dying during the early 1920s from wounds sustained during the First World War. Frank Wood, whom he took into partnership after the close of the war, supervised the contract during its final stages — a series of buildings exuding a relaxed, refined air grouped around a huge, central lawn. The individual halls — Buchanan, Carlyle, Darroch, Playfair and Balfour — are generally characterised by graceful bow windows, advanced, gabled porches (rather Dutch in appearance), swelling mansard roofs with plain and decorative dormers to the attic behind, and many, generous, small-paned windows. Darroch and Carlyle — without bow windows

— are linked by a single storey pavilion block; symmetrical, with bulbous bays, and set behind a balustraded garden area. The campus, redolent as it is of Lorimer's work, is an attractive example of work created in a good Scots idiom.

Crosslee Mills, Renfrewshire

1917

Crosslee Mills, Houston, Renfrewshire
William McLennan

No two buildings could be less alike than St. Matthew's Church of Scotland in Paisley (1908), and the former Crosslee Mills near Houston in Renfrewshire; yet, both were products of the fertile mind of William McLennan. Originally used as a factory for the manufacture of cordite, the latter building was erected in 'in-situ' reinforced concrete, with great expanses of glazing stretching between externally expressed octagonal perimeter columns. Closely centred concrete fins project from the coarsely shuttered facade to support cantilevered walkways at first floor and roof level, the latter flat, and accessible via a bridge from the rear of the steeply falling site. At ground level, huge doorways open onto a platform beneath which passes a narrow river. The starkness of the exterior is dramatically relieved by the sudden and daring cantilever of one section of the first floor, out over this rushing water. While essentially uncompromising and utilitarian, the architecture of this building is not without a certain rugged, honest appeal — the bare concrete unpainted, unadorned and unabashed.

1918

Aircraft Hangars, Old Airfield, Montrose
Architect unknown

The former airfield at Montrose is dotted with huge hangars, of which easily the most interesting are the oldest — a pair of vast timber-built shells. Here, an old and well-tried technology was adopted for a new use — closely spaced roof trusses bearing onto simple timber posts, with the horizontally boarded walls braced on the exterior by bolted timber buttresses seated in concrete pads.

Aircraft Hangars, Montrose

Windows are high, large and evenly positioned; the outside is clad in a dark building felt, tarred in places. At either end of each hangar is a simple, functional framework which protrudes at the sides to accommodate the sliding motion of the great doors. Despite their somewhat weatherbeaten appearance, the hangars have an unexpected appeal — born largely out of the rationale of the construction, and the simplicity of the structure. At the time of writing, they await dismantling and re-erection at Bo'ness.

Rosyth Garden Village, Fife

1919

Rosyth Garden Village, Fife
A H Mottram/Greig and Fairbairn

Shortly after the republication, in 1902, of his *Garden Cities of Tomorrow*, Ebenezer Howard formed a Garden City syndicate with, as its chief architects and planners, the partnership of Barry Parker and Raymond Unwin. Letchworth Garden City in Hertfordshire was begun by the company in 1904, although almost a decade elapsed before a similar such venture was proposed for the 'New Town' at Rosyth. A H Mottram, a pupil of Unwin, came to Scotland to oversee the work at Rosyth, although the first 150 houses were built to the designs of Greig and Fairbairn of Edinburgh. By 1919, however, a substantial number of houses had been erected, many to Mottram's designs. Shops, schools, clubs and churches were gradually added over a period of years. The informal layout of the town roughly accords with Howard's original visionary notion of a new village for the working class; that is, a central park surrounded by rings of housing, with an outer belt — within which industry and commerce were confined — encircling the whole. At Rosyth, the park is indeed central, with Queensferry Road acting as the main thoroughfare on either side of which spread crescents and curves dotted with neat little houses with tree-lined gardens. This housing — some harled, others brick, some tiled, others slated — is in need of a little attention. Happily, the Scottish Special Housing Association, successor of the Scottish National Housing Company Ltd. (whose incentive it was to begin the development) have undertaken to maintain this pleasant garden suburb.

1920

'Cour', Kintyre, Argyllshire
Oliver Hill

Oliver Hill was a colourful character, whose practice was at its most prolific during the 1930s when he designed a number of fine buildings in the International Style. These were not wholly typical of his career, however, since he had the ability to move from one idiom to another with formidable ease — responding to each commission in the manner he thought best suited to it; a persuasive architect, who gave " his clients what they want, and also what he wants them to want . . .". The great mound of stone and slate that is the mansion of 'Cour' on the Argyllshire peninsula of Kintyre, was one of Hill's first large post-war buildings — an impressive pile which errs slightly on the side of English medievalism, and whose rolling roof might have been better expressed in thatch; but a friendly house, and cosy in its niche in the landscape. It is sunk low in the grounds when seen from the approach road, but with terraces and steps to increase its stature as the site falls away to the Kilbrannan Sound. There is a romantic, leisurely sprawl to it, as it sweeps and curves around a predominantly 'L'-shaped plan, full of slit windows, arches, grand battered chimneys and lead-topped bays. Scottish it is not, or not quite, but a fitting response to a splendid Scottish site and the less than splendid Scottish climate it is, and as such has a permanence and suitability which belies its relative youth.

'Cour', Kintyre

1921

War Memorial and Cowdray Hall, Schoolhill, Aberdeen
A Marshall MacKenzie

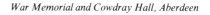

The severe quadrant corner of Aberdeen's War Memorial was initially designed as the setting for a memorial to Edward VII, but in view of the fact that construction of this addition to the Art Gallery did not commence until well after the close of the war, its purpose was altered accordingly. The sweeping concave curve of the facade, behind which is housed a dome-topped memorial court, is given depth by a Corinthian colonnade; six slender columns throwing gaunt shadows onto the stark surface of the wall behind. Within the curve — at either end of which are located entrances, one to the adjacent Cowdray Hall, and the other to the memorial court itself — sits a handsome, snooty lion, carved by W McMillan. The solemnity of the corner is heightened by the unrelieved use of a pale grey granite, in contrast to the return of the facade where pilasters and pediment are picked out in a rosy red stone. The architect for both the Art Gallery (1885) and these subsequent extensions, was A Marshall MacKenzie — showing here a restraint which was not evident in his earlier work at Marischal College (1900)!

War Memorial and Cowdray Hall, Aberdeen

Zoology Building, Glasgow University, Glasgow

1922

Zoology Building, Glasgow University, Glasgow
Sir John James Burnet with Norman A Dick

Shortly before construction commenced on the Memorial Chapel (1923–27) designed for the University of Glasgow by Sir J J Burnet, work began on another of his projects for the same client — the Zoology Building off University Avenue. Deceptive in scale — not nearly so diminutive as the entrance facade suggests — the bulk of the building is clothed in a precise, channelled ashlar, with a jaunty louvred cupola located to the left of the entrance, and squat dwarf pilasters appearing at first floor level on the gable of

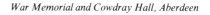

the laboratory block. Laboratories and lecture theatre are each given individual expression in this adventurous composition: the first housed behind a substantially glazed wall mullioned in a modern, twentieth century manner; the other lit by windows whose sill level drops with the rake of the auditorium floor inside. Beyond this facade stretches a great screen wall with two gaunt, blind windows featuring elongated keystones. While Burnet is suspected of having suppressed his natural flair in the design of the chapel (in order that the building appeared sympathetic to Scott's original aesthetic) the Zoology building — designed in association with Norman A Dick — shows better his style and design ability.

Arches, City Chambers extension, John Street, Glasgow
Watson Salmond and Gray

Glasgow's City Chambers (1883) are linked to an eastern extension (later by some forty years and almost as extensive as the original) by an exceptional pair of arches, through and under which pass corridors connecting the two buildings. French Renaissance in style, the arches and extension were designed

Arches, City Chambers, Glasgow

in response to an open competition staged in 1913, although construction work was delayed until after the war. The arches, each with a main, central opening flanked by smaller, pedestrian passages, feature coupled Ionic columns set on pale granite bases and supporting decorative urns and shallow arched pediments. There is a great deal of elaborate carving and, extraordinarily still intact, six fine period lamps suspended from the underside of each of the openings. Designed by John Watson of the local firm Watson, Salmond and Gray, the knitting together of this municipal complex — old building and newer — is aided in no small way by these arches, the language of which responds equally well to either building.

Scottish National War Memorial, Edinburgh

1924

Scottish National War Memorial, Edinburgh Castle, Edinburgh
Sir Robert Lorimer

Robert Lorimer's last major commission was to design the National War Memorial at Edinburgh Castle. It was a prolonged exercise for the architect, and one which ended in compromise for, in the face of some concern from the appointed committee over the possible disruption of the familiar castle silhouette, Lorimer was compelled to make use of an existing barracks building centred on the Castle Rock. Thus, to the repaired and remodelled shell of the older structure, he added a south-facing porch and a sturdy, sixteenth century Scottish chapel apse to the north. Both were convincingly allied to the original building through the use of a stone from Northumberland which was found to be a good match. The rugged appearance of this masonry, smooth only in and around niches, arches and windows, allows the building to sit comfortably on the crest of the site, with the ragged face of the once volcanic rock protruding through the floor of the shrine. Memorials of every size and shape were accommodated within the gallery; one each for the Scottish regiments, and with stained glass windows, insignia, friezes and sculpture depicting various aspects of the war. Begun in 1923, the building was inaugurated by the Prince of Wales in 1927, its completion as fitting a tribute to the many Scots who fell during the First World War, as it was to the architect who had nursed the project through to the end.

Winter Gardens Pavilion, Rothesay

1925

Winter Gardens Pavilion, Victoria Street, Rothesay, Bute
Alex Stephen

Rothesay's frivolous Winter Gardens Pavilion is not, as its appearance suggests, Victorian in origin, but was built during the 1920s, from which time — until recently — it served as the prime venue for summer entertainment on the island. Situated at the head of the pier, the building began life as a small bandstand on the esplanade, to which were added, around 1924, a low circular auditorium and dressing rooms. The materials used in the construction of the building were of a light, modern nature, designed to create a colourful, festive atmosphere; seaside architecture in an appropriately light-hearted vein. Yet, despite the fairy lights strung between the balcony lamp-standards, and over the pert little entrance towers with their pagoda roofs, the pavilion is a surprisingly serious essay in engineering, with an extremely elegant section composed of riveted ribs widening from a solid section at the apex to a skeletal series of loops formed within the outline of the steel at the supports. Around the perimeter of the dome runs a concrete balcony with an intricate wrought-iron balustrade. Glazing at ground floor level is of obscured glass with a spreading patent-glazed awning over. Interestingly, the Rothesay Winter Gardens Pavilion has the same exotic, curious air as Wemyss Bay Station — designed some twenty years earlier and only a ferry trip away.

200 St. Vincent Street, Glasgow

1926

200 St. Vincent Street, Blythswood, Glasgow
Sir John James Burnet with Norman A Dick

St. Vincent Street in Glasgow can boast of more than a few of the city's finest buildings, ranking high amongst which is the former North British and Mercantile Building at No. 200. Designed by Sir J J Burnet in 1926, in association with his Scottish-based partner Norman A Dick, this severe box of a building (virtually a cube) was one of the last major designs on which the elder architect worked personally. The exterior is quite stark, although by no means starved of detail, with very little sculpture and applied decoration; a monolithic block of stone lowered onto the site, into which comparatively small windows have been punched at regular intervals, and around the base of which runs an arcade. These ground and first floor arches are not glazed to any great extent, but mostly infilled with stone, and coupled by twin engaged columns.

Simple, statuesque and a superb corner-piece, nine or ten loadbearing storeys more would have provided Glasgow with its very own version of the Monadnock Building in Chicago (Burnham and Root, 1891), which Burnet is likely to have seen on his tour of America in 1896.

1927

St. Conan's Kirk, Loch Awe, Argyllshire
Walter Douglas Campbell

The most scenic stretch of Loch Awe, along which can be found St. Conan's Kirk, lies between the site of Kilchurn Castle and the mouth of the Pass of Brander. Clinging tenaciously to the south-facing hillside at the foot of which it sits, this remarkable church is stylistically far removed from the architecture of the period during which it was completed. The building, as it stands today, grew up around a smaller church which was incorporated into the nave of the present structure, begun in 1907. Walter Douglas Campbell of Blythswood, having purchased the nearby island of Innischonain, devoted the latter part of his life to the erection of the building, ostensibly to relieve his mother of the lengthy trip to the parish church at Dalmally. Work stopped during the First World War, in addition to which progress was ponderously slow, with the building completed long after Campbell's death in 1914 and only consecrated

St. Conan's Kirk, Loch Awe

as recently as 1930. Great grey, yellow and red boulders were rolled down to the site where they were individually split and shaped. These were then piled up and delicately carved, particularly on the south front, where there are fern-like forms on the smaller of the two towers, a row of beady-eyed owls around the entrance archway, and three splendid buttresses bolstered against the retaining walls. Particularly attractive is the gaily patterned leadwork on the cloister roofs, the beautifully fashioned lead gargoyles — a dog and two hares chasing each other across the west facade — and the internal timberwork, all supervised by Campbell and his sister Helen. This building, which gives much pleasure to its many visitors, constitutes a great personal endeavour, and is architecture on an elevated plane.

1928

Home Farm Dairy, Kinfauns
Sir Robert Lorimer

Kinfauns lies east of Perth, en route to Dundee and with forest, castle and associated farms. If the dairy built in the grounds of the Home Farm there represents one of Lorimer's smallest commissions, it was also one of his last — completed in the year before his death, which occurred in September 1929. The appeal of this little building lies in its simplicity, coupled with the unexpected size of the roof. It comprises an octagon linked to a gabled, rectangular room, all in large, fairy regular blocks of rough-hewn stone. Hovering above this is a bulbous, bluebell-shaped slate roof supported at its edges by simple timber posts. While this roof has all the spreading, curving characteristics of which Lorimer made such frequent use, it also bears more than a passing similarity to the safari helmet which his friend and contemporary Sir Edwin Lutyens was often seen to wear. It is amusing to speculate that this may have been an indirect source of inspiration to the Scottish architect . . .

Home Farm Dairy, Kinfauns

1929

Cochrane Park Hall, Stirling Road, Alva
William Kerr

The Cochrane Park Hall in Alva, while curiously detailed, is a fetching composition which mimics rather well the rolling, sweeping contours of the surrounding landscape. Looking less towards the uncluttered modernism of the thirties than it does back, to the architecture of Voysey and Baillie-Scott, the

Cochrane Park Hall, Alva

pavilion — tall for a single storey structure — was designed by a locally based architect, William Kerr. There is a Lorimeresque quality about the building, most apparent in the manner in which the roof has been used to bind together a slightly irregular 'H'-shaped plan; in fact, the building shares some of the features which make the Home Farm Dairy at Kinfauns (1928) so picturesque. Up top, there is an elongated cupola, centred above a fanciful, gabled entrance porch on either side of which stretch loggias — roofed over and with timber Doric posts. White harled, and more roof than walls or windows, this little building certainly deserves more than a passing glance.

India Tyre and Rubber Factory, Inchinnan

1930

India Tyre and Rubber Factory, Greenock Road, Inchinnan
Wallis Gilbert and Partners

One of the most arresting architectural applications of the Art Deco style in Britain was the Firestone Factory on the Great West Road in London (1929). The demolition, in 1980, of its exotic central pavilion greatly increases the value of the still extant India Tyre and Rubber Company's factory at Inchinnan, similar in form and finish and designed by the same firm of Wallis, Gilbert and Partners. Opened in April 1930, the splendid white stuccoed exterior of the main office building on Greenock Road is an unusual and wholly unexpected feature of the area. John Wallis once advised that, "a little money wisely spent in the incorporation of some form of decoration, especially colour, was not money wasted. It had a psychological effect on the worker . . . (and) . . . was good advertisement." Hence, green, red and black tiles have been judiciously applied to the facade to enliven its appearance, and a wealth of colour and fine metalwork concentrated around the main entrance. Wallis tackled each commission anew, and so, although the entrance to the Inchinnan building clearly had its origins in that at Firestone, the former is finished in green and a pinky-red, whereas gold and a deep blue predominated around the doorway of the earlier factory. Ironically, the future of the Inchinnan complex is currently uncertain.

#

St. Anne's RC Church, 10 Whitevale Street, Dennistoun, Glasgow
Gillespie Kidd and Coia

The most significant and sizeable contribution made to the development of Scottish church architecture since the 1930s can be attributed to the Glasgow firm of Gillespie Kidd and Coia. St. Anne's Roman Catholic Church in Dennistoun represents the first opportunity Jack Coia had to make known his skills as a designer. The erection of the building coincided with a growing awareness in Britain of the liturgical movement, ie with the need to revise the established ritual of worship in the Church and to devise means of reinterpreting the traditions of church architecture to accommodate such changes. Thus, Coia abandoned the traditional plan-type in favour of a generous vaulted space in the form of a Latin cross, and in so doing made "a move towards the concept of unencumbered space, with clear vision throughout from all points of the church". The entrance facade, placed behind

St. Anne's RC Church, Dennistoun, Glasgow

a screen wall with railings of extraordinary complexity, is an early Italian Renaissance composition executed in modern materials — a red facing brick with beautifully worked stone dressings, voluptuous stone and brick flanking scrolls, unusual entrance archways with vaguely Celtic encrustations, and slightly mannered brick-on-edge ribs radiating out around the top of the presbytery windows and the arcaded aisles. St. Anne's, then, was a church built in materials with which community and congregation were familiar, on a scale to which they could relate, and in a language they were able to understand.

1932

Reid Memorial Church, Blackford Avenue, Edinburgh
Leslie Grahame Thomson

At the intersection of Blackford Avenue, Charterhall Road and West Savile Terrace in Edinburgh stands the elegant Reid Memorial Church, designed by Leslie Grahame Thomson in 1932, but belonging firmly to the period during which architects such as Robert Lorimer, John Kinross and Reginald Fairlie each practised their own versions of a Scots revival style. Thomson's church comes closest to the work of Lorimer, daintily detailed and making effective use of the contrast between dressed and rough-hewn stone. The keynote of the main body of the church is loftiness — the nave long and slim and very bright. To the north of the complex is an attractive gateway with some rather fanciful ironwork — the arch providing the only peak in a stone wall created out of

Reid Memorial Church, Edinburgh

troughs. To the east are some fine cloister-like buildings and little ogee roofs dotted around. Edinburgh succumbed to the attractions of the International Style not long after the completion of this dapper, Edwardian building, which was, in effect, a "virtuoso performance in a style . . . in its last throws".

46a Dick Place, Edinburgh

1933

46a Dick Place, Edinburgh
Kininmonth and Spence

The *leitmotiv* of 'modern' domestic (and other) architecture during the 1930s was commonly a combination of flat roof, white rendered walls and metal-framed, horizontal windows. An early example of this aesthetic in Edinburgh can be found at 46a Dick Place, in the house designed by and for Sir William Kininmonth in 1933. 'More or less converted by Corbusier' by 1930, the architect — in collaboration with a young Basil Spence — produced a tightly planned scheme displaying more than a few of the hallmarks of the International Style; a generous roof terrace, a token cantilevered canopy, and a graceful, curving lounge facade largely occupied by a screen of glass swept round in a staccato burst of mullions. Here, however, the windows are timber-framed and vertical with a vengeance! Peeping out from behind dense garden foliage, the house remained incomplete until after the Second World War, when additional accommodation and a studio space were located to the rear. Kininmonth still lives in this stylish white house, which he cites as one of the few instances on which he and Spence were given the opportunity to practise a 'modern' architecture together.

1934

St. Andrew's House, Calton Hill, Edinburgh
Thomas S Tait

Anchored firmly to the slope on which once sat Edinburgh's Calton Jail, St. Andrew's House (until recently the headquarters of government administration in Scotland) is an assertive, monumental mass — bastion-like not benevolent — but enlivened by some fine period detailing. Sprawling on plan, and serious by nature, the building is appropriately impressive, with the administration arms of the north facade gaining in height and stature as they approach the powerful pillared entrance front. Here, on either side of two magnificent bronze doors are stubby columns with curious fluted capitals and,

St. Andrew's House, Edinburgh

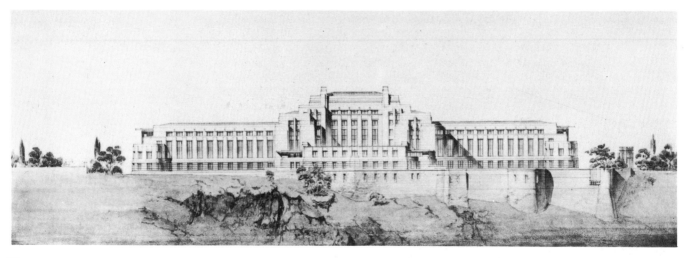

above these, an enormous carving of the Royal Coat of Arms of Scotland. Built in a pale Creetown granite, the solidity of the building is momentarily relieved by the glazed stairtowers which, with their oversailing eaves, mark secondary entrances to the complex. Thomas S Tait (of Sir John Burnet, Tait and Lorne), one of Scotland's finest inter-war architects, was responsible for the design of this striking composition.

1935

Royal Bank of Scotland, 30 Bothwell Street, Glasgow
James Miller

Pokey-eyed and powerful, James Miller's Royal Bank of Scotland (formerly the National Commercial Bank) occupies a small site at the junction of Glasgow's Bothwell Street and Wellington Street. It is one of the smallest and finest of a series of American-influenced commercial buildings in the city which make use of a giant order with an infill of glass and cast-metal panels. Here, the order is Corinthian, with two gleaming Portland stone columns soaring up from a polished plinth to dominate the huge void created on the entrance facade. Up top, at roof level, there is no cornice, only a scarcely detectable band of incised ornament. This, coupled with the Art Deco-inspired sculpted panels by Gilbert Bays, earmark the building as a product of the thirties period. It is generally thought that Miller, in the design of his later and better works, relied heavily on the assistance of Richard M. Gunn, a very able architect.

Royal Bank of Scotland, Glasgow

1936

'Glasgow Herald' Building, 163 Albion Street, Glasgow
Sir E Owen Williams

The angular good looks of the former *Daily Express* building in Glasgow remain almost perfectly preserved in a showcase of metal-framed ribbon glazing and polished black glass. These Albion Street offices, similar in

'Glasgow Herald' Building, Glasgow

construction and appearance to the Fleet Street headquarters of the newspaper group (1932), were designed by the engineer-architect Sir E Owen Williams, who is best remembered for the seminal Boots Factory in Nottinghamshire (1930). The factory, while highly influential, had a functional ruthlessness about it, which he succeeded in refining in the design of the Glasgow building. It is considerably less demonstrative of its structure, although most of the ground floor is recessed beneath expressed concrete cantilevers. Thus, the absence of a solid base enhances the effect of lightness created by the upper floors. The precise, simple proportions of the block — now used in the production of the *Glasgow Herald* — were upset when additional accommodation was erected on the roof.

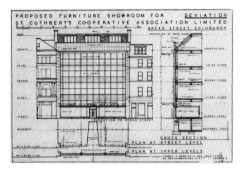

St. Cuthbert's Co-operative, Edinburgh

1937

St. Cuthbert's Co-operative, 22-34 Bread Street, Edinburgh
T Waller Marwick

Edinburgh's earliest example of the curtain-walling technique — the Bread Street elevation of the St. Cuthbert's Co-operative building — has none of the hierarchical gradation evident in the fenestration of neighbouring facades. Instead, it is a regularly patterned wall of glass, with a widely spaced structural frame (steel clad in pale coloured concrete) once visible behind a smaller chequered grid of bronze astragals. These astragals are briefly attached to stanchions and downstand beams by little lugs — their tenuous grip on the concrete hidden by the pastel colours in which the facade has been unflatteringly painted. Designed by T Waller Marwick on a north facing site, the building — deep and narrow and intended for the display of a wide range of goods including furniture, china and glass — was an interesting and innovative addition to the city's streetscape. Particularly cunning, with regard to drawing customers into the store, was the deep, wedge-shaped entrance at ground level; glazed on both sides and working its way back through a third of the building before reaching the entrance doors!

1938

Empire Exhibition, Bellahouston Park, Glasgow (demolished)
Thomas S Tait

Of the four open-air exhibitions staged in Glasgow since 1888, the last — the Empire Exhibition of 1938 — was the largest and finest. The man responsible for devising the overall layout at Bellahouston Park, and for the detailing of many of the individual pavilions erected there, was Thomas S Tait, architect of one of the most prestigious works designed in Scotland during the 1930s — Edinburgh's St. Andrew's House (1934). The object of the exhibition was twofold: to promote British products and encourage trade, and to depict the progress of the Empire. To this end, and bearing in mind the depression evident in the host city in particular, Tait had built a gleaming symbol of optimism, a 300 foot high observation tower sited on the crest of Bellahouston Hill — a striking stepped edifice rising out of dense greenery and whose sleek, stylised profile defied the incessant rain which dogged the exhibition for its duration. If the tower was the most prominent feature of the display, then the Garden Club — designed by Tait in collaboration with T Waller Marwick — was the most popular. Quite apart from the delight with which it was greeted by the public, it was a remarkably graceful architectural statement; on plan, a sequence of flowing curves and volutes; three dimensionally, a dramatic and elegant advertisement for Thirties modernism. The demolition of this, the tower, and all but one of the other, equally original palaces and pavilions, robbed Glasgow of one of its most enjoyable architectural displays.

Empire Exhibition, Glasgow

1939

Glasgow University Reading Room, University Avenue, Glasgow
T Harold Hughes and D S R Waugh

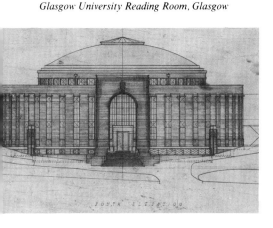

Glasgow University Reading Room, Glasgow

If purity of form mattered more than surface modelling during the thirties, then St. Andrew's House in Edinburgh (1934) and Glasgow University's Reading Room are good examples of this tenet. Seemingly large when viewed in isolation (but quite small beside T L Watson's Wellington Church of 1883) this latter building, a domed rotunda located on a generous site on University Avenue, was designed to permit maximum supervision of the reading room using a minimum of staff. Hence, reading stations are arranged on a radial layout, at the centre of which is an enquiries desk. The impressive brick-clad entrance arch straddles a curving, glazed staircase which, with the vertical strip windows regularly spaced around the circumference of the building, emits light during the evening, when the facilities are most in use. Built in 1939, and designed by T Harold Hughes and D S R Waugh, the construction of the Reading Room coincided with the commencement of the University's Chemistry Building; by the same architects and with a splendid, dynamic glazed staircase tower.

1940 – 45

Italian Chapel, Lamb Holm, Orkney
Identity of architects unknown

Very little architecture of any real merit emerged during the Second World War. Buildings were necessarily of a utilitarian nature, although this did not preclude improvisation and inspiration giving rise to the occasional gem. The Italian Chapel on Lamb Holm in Orkney was built from a nissen hut, plaster, assorted scrap material, iron, concrete and stone by Italian prisoners of war, captured during the North African conflict of 1940–1943 and employed in the construction of causeways (the 'Churchill Barrier') linking Mainland to South Ronaldsay. Essentially an entrance facade complete with columnar porch,

Italian Chapel, Lamb Holm, Orkney

flanking piers, lancet windows, crockets and bell, the chapel has evidently been painstakingly composed and constructed, with the beautiful interior carefully painted to give the illusion of solidity and permanance, and to lend richness to the basic materials used. This patient endeavour succeeded in producing a very moving piece of architecture.

NCR Factory, Dundee

1946

NCR Factory, Camperdown Park, Dundee
Bennet, Beard and Wilkins

The revival of Scottish industry was commenced with a vengeance almost immediately after the cessation of the Second World War. Of the industrial estates created, the first in Scotland to attract an American company was the Kingsway Industrial Estate on the outskirts of Dundee. Here, National Cash Register established themselves in an elegant, yellow brick building designed by Bennet, Beard and Wilkins of London. Built in Camperdown Park, the factory stretches interminably in two directions, the main facade long and low and pierced by small windows at ground floor level. Features are made of the entrance block — higher, and with an asymmetrically placed opening — and of a flat-roofed section, protruding, fully glazed and lending transparency to an almost impregnable elevation. Elsewhere, little portholes dot the exterior. Although the great spreads of brickwork used give the factory a gritty, practical air, it is pleasantly proportioned and with an arresting simplicity. At present, it is unoccupied.

1947

Timex Factory, Dryburgh Estate, Dundee
Bennet, Beard and Wilkins

Begun in parallel with the NCR Factory (1946) and designed by the same architects, the US Time (Timex) building — sited atop an undulating hillside on the Dryburgh Estate — was rapidly occupied on completion by the second

Timex Factory, Dundee

American company to be attracted to the Tayside region. The building has much in common with NCR — long, (really long, seeming to extend indefinitely in the direction of a nearby woodland) low, flat roofed and utterly uncomplicated. Again, the predominant material used in the construction of the factory was a yellowish brick. Here, however, the entrance is highlighted in a red sandstone, with an occasional stone dressing making an appearance on the main elevation. From the street passing by the foot of the estate this south facade can be detected lurking on the horizon, a subtly irregular rhythm of closely crammed windows racing off to the west and the woods. Like the NCR complex, it is the stylish, casual simplicity of the Timex factory which so appeals.

Fountainbridge Telephone Exchange, Edinburgh

1948

Telephone Exchange, 116 Fountainbridge, Edinburgh
PSA Department of the Environment (then Ministry of Works)

Exhibiting the same simple, solid geometry which typifies so many buildings of the period, Edinburgh's Fountainbridge Telephone Exchange is a weighty, stone-clad structure sited in a somewhat determined fashion on the corner of Gardner's Crescent and Fountainbridge. The entrance, located at the base of an asymmetrically glazed stairtower, shelters between the beckoning curve of the adjacent administration block and the gaunt east wall of the switch gear and apparatus rooms. This latter, taller wing juts confidently forward from the main body of the building — slender steel columns (cased in concrete and finished in stone) separating three huge vertical strips of glazing on the south facade. These glazed indents, repeated on the east and west, contrast with and complement the more conventional fenestration of the office wing, the graceful curve of which serves to guide the building around the corner.

1949

The Inch, Housing and Community Development, Gilmerton Road, Edinburgh
David Stratton Davis

The Inch, Edinburgh

The Inch, a fine crow-stepped and harled 17th Century mansion house, stands in what was formerly a 215 acre expanse of agricultural land in the Liberton area of Edinburgh. Now used as a community centre, the conversion of the building formed part of the competition-winning proposals for the development of the site, made in 1946 by the Gloucester architect David Stratton Davis. Built for the then Edinburgh Corporation, the housing, concentrated to the east and south of The Inch, adopts an informal layout which is dictated largely by the steep fall of the land to the north. The majority of the buildings — a combination of two and three-storey blocks — are finished in white or tinted cement stucco, have dainty, Regency style porches, and are roofed in either copper or Scots slates. Simple balconies and bay windows also feature throughout the scheme. Planned on a garden city layout, with several schools and a church close by, the development represents the direction the Corporation had elected to pursue in their provision of housing and community estates in the city.

1950

Fishermen's Houses, Lamer Street, Dunbar
Sir Basil Spence

The demolition of various derelict properties in the harbour area of Dunbar gave the Town Council the opportunity of increasing the accommodation available at the time for fishermen and their families. The housing thus provided, which was grouped around the existing Lifeboat House and a terraced row of dwellings completed in 1936, was designed by Basil Spence, and combined three, four, and sometimes five apartment single-storey flats at ground level, with two-storey houses which were located above these, and

Fishermen's Houses, Dunbar

95

reached via external balconies. Contemporary in both layout and manner (the fenestration anything but traditional), the overall character of the scheme is still sufficiently evocative of the spirit of the area to allow it to sit comfortably in the harbour surrounds. As if to root the buildings there, the lower levels of the houses are finished in the pinky-red local stone, while upper floors are clad in brick with a colour-washed roughcast coating, and roofs finished in cheerful red pantiles.

Natural Philosophy Building, Glasgow University, Glasgow

Extensions, Natural Philosophy Building, Glasgow University, Glasgow
Sir Basil Spence with Glover and Ferguson

Built to house a 300 million volt synchrotron (the largest in Europe at the time of installation), the first extension to Glasgow University's original Natural Philosophy building (1907) was completed in 1951. Designed to take best advantage of a restricted site — hemmed in by the Chemistry, Botany and Zoology complexes — the building had to house the particle accelerator underground, from where the beam could be directed into fifteen feet of concrete and where radiation, noise and vibration could be contained. To this end, a 150 ton sliding door was located over the top of the synchrotron. In 1959, a teaching wing linking this research block with its predecessor completed the scheme. The junction between the two phases, both designed by Sir Basil Spence and Partners, is barely perceptible, the west facade characterised by a first floor with an expressed framed construction separating a textured Blaxter stone base and upper floors clad in a smooth Portland stone. The main entrance, located on the corner of the earlier block, is a very pleasant space reached via a generous flight of stairs and featuring a display area poking out from the intersection between north and west wings.

Pollock Halls of Residence, Dalkeith Road, Edinburgh
Rowand Anderson, Kininmonth and Paul

Pollock Halls of Residence, Edinburgh

Sidling around the base of Arthur's Seat, Edinburgh University's Pollock Halls of Residence comprise two semi-enclosed courtyards facing one another across a quadrangle and, nearby, a larger courtyard at the heart of which is a dining hall. The accommodation blocks wrapped around these landscaped areas are domestic in scale and appearance, with shallow copper-clad roofs and an economical use of warmly tinted renders. A collegiate atmosphere is achieved,

however, through the introduction of cloisters at ground floor level — the shallow, alternating arches encircling one of the courtyards strangely reminiscent of the quayside arcades of Jesse Hartley's Albert Dock warehouses in Liverpool (1845). Designed by Sir William Kininmonth, the scheme also features some dainty Swedish-influenced lantern towers.

1953

Health Centre, Sighthill, Edinburgh
R Gardner-Medwin

The first development of its kind to be undertaken in Scotland, the Sighthill Health Centre was a "bright and much discussed young thing among the younger generations after the war". Stretched out around a garden courtyard, three of the four wings — housing a medical unit, a joint services and X-Ray unit, and a child welfare centre — are single storey, copper roofed and brick clad. The north wing, in which are located administrative offices and a dental

Sighthill Health Centre, Edinburgh

clinic, comprises a basement and two floors — each level individually expressed in a different cladding material. The entrance, tucked beneath the pillar-supported north-west front, opens into a stylish foyer space, with curved reception area and an elegant, spiralling concrete staircase. This is visible on the north facade, rising up behind a screen of glazing; a graceful, natural foil to the jutting, geometric bay windows which enlarge the first floor dental surgeries. The centre was designed by Robert Gardner-Medwin while chief architect for the Department of Health.

1954

Rothes Colliery, Thornton
Egon Riss

Egon Riss brought drama to the industrial architecture of the Scottish division of the National Coal Board during its post-war development of new collieries. Rothes Colliery, initiated by the Fife Coal Company Ltd., and the last major

Rothes Colliery, Thornton

mining project in the country to be advanced under private enterprise, is characterised by an elongated glazed spine (which housed the car circulation hall) and two gaunt, 190 foot high towers, whose stark profiles throw huge enveloping shadows over the sparse Kirkcaldy landscape. Equipped with powerful Koepe winders, the towers — each slightly swollen at the base — are built of reinforced concrete, but extensively glazed and thus relatively light in appearance. The surface complex also included an administration centre and a baths building, both marked by the same expressive combination of exposed concrete and glass, and linked by a concrete loggia. Originally begun to mine the deep seams north of Kirkcaldy, and to produce a daily output of 5,000 tons of coal, Rothes was closed in May 1962, an unusual geological pattern having emerged which made economical working impossible.

Vale of Leven Hospital, Alexandria

1955

Vale of Leven Hospital, Alexandria
John Keppie and Henderson and J L Gleave

During the 1950s and early 60s, construction work in Scotland was concentrated largely on the development of new towns, schools, multi-storey housing and hospitals. In this last category, the Vale of Leven Hospital in Dunbartonshire was the first entirely new hospital to be completed in Britain after the war. The complex, designed by J L Gleave, shelters in what was formerly an agricultural valley south of Loch Lomond; a long, irregularly shaped brick-built services and circulation spine travelling the north/south axis of the site, and sprouting prefabricated 'accommodation' units along its length. The appearance of the hospital was dictated by the need to allow future expansion, and to maintain a profile low and expansive enough to guarantee light and shelter to every aspect of the scheme. Hence, the architecture relies for effect on the contrast between the small-windowed permanence of the services backbone and the lightness and transparency of the ward blocks; these defined by the strong verticality of regularly spaced concrete mullions infilled with a seemingly random pattern of glazed and cedar-boarded panels. These rapidly assembled materials are common to ward blocks, theatre buildings and nurses' quarters, all designed as 100ft × 40ft rectangular blocks capable of supporting a further, third floor if necessary.

1956

Turnhouse Airport, Edinburgh
Robert Matthew, Johnson-Marshall and Partners

Sir Robert Matthew resumed work in Scotland in 1953, after having designed the Royal Festival Hall (1951) on London's South Bank while with the LCC's Architects Department. He brought the same meticulous attention to detail to the first phase of Edinburgh's Turnhouse Airport; completed in 1956 and copiously clad in the timber weatherboarding which so typifies the architecture of the period. Extended twice before being usurped by the present Edinburgh

Turnhouse Airport, Edinburgh

Airport (opened in 1977 and by the same firm of architects), the original terminal building was a modestly dimensioned structure which nonetheless easily and effectively accommodated a complex interrelationship of circulatory and administrative functions, while catering splendidly for passengers and staff with an attractive buffet space and generous roof terrace. A deceptively simple series of interpenetrating volumes, the interior featured a wealth of individually designed fittings — lamps, clocks, ironmongery, notice boards, light fittings, furniture and even rugs. The buildings, handling over 625,000 passengers by the mid sixties, are now used for air cargo.

1957

St. Paul's R C Church, Glenrothes, Fife
Gillespie Kidd and Coia

A visible shift occurred in the ecclesiastical work of Gillespie Kidd and Coia around the mid fifties. The completion of St. Paul's Roman Catholic Church in June of 1958 marked a departure from the traditionally inspired layout and appearance of buildings such as St. Anne's in Dennistoun (1931), and the unveiling of a refreshing, economical severity of form. The first Roman Catholic church to be built in the New Town of Glenrothes, St. Paul's is a fairly bald, bold statement — smooth, white, windowless walls enclosing a fan-shaped church above the sanctuary of which rises a tower whose glazed west wall floods the high altar and its unusual bronze cross with white light. The random mullioned effect of this facade is repeated at a lower level on the main entrance wall, where the glass is both clear and coloured, and contained in satisfyingly solid timber framing. A drum-like hall, designed to accentuate the brusque geometrical nature of the church proper was never built, but there is a low, flat-roofed presbytery linked to the main building. In its stark simplicity and frankly ruthless abandon of decorative features, St. Paul's stood as an exciting precursor of the scores of buildings which the firm were to design in a similar genre.

St. Paul's R C Church, Fife

1958

'Avisfield', Cramond Road North, Edinburgh
Morris and Steedman

The flat roof may no longer be fashionable, and indeed was never particularly successful, but it was used to undeniably good effect at 'Avisfield', the first house to be built by the Edinburgh firm of Morris and Steedman. Here, the main criterion was to capture any available sunshine, and to this end a spacious

exterior courtyard was created, enclosed on two sides by the 'L' shape of the house and on the others by a high stone wall. The privacy and shelter thus afforded the space, coupled with the generous glazing of the rooms around, ensured that the courtyard became a recognisable extension of the interior. Visibly influenced by the work of the American Frank Lloyd Wright and the Viennese architect Richard Neutra, the house has a stone feature chimney and a large inglenook fireplace at the heart of the living area. The elegant flat roof, which actually comprises two interpenetrating rectangular planes, the lower over the garage, lends this attractive, stylish house a quiet and unassuming air.

'Avisfield', Edinburgh

St. Mark's Catholic Church, Edinburgh

1959

St. Mark's Catholic Church, Oxgangs Avenue, Edinburgh
Peter Whiston

Rising confidently above the west elevation of St. Mark's Catholic Church in Edinburgh is a bold timber cross, outlined in red against a background of glazing, and framed within the gable of a steeply pitched roof. Below this prominent feature, and decreasing in height with the barely perceptible fall of the site, sit the presbytery and other ancillary buildings — trimly detailed and flat roofed. The roof of the presbytery, which defines a courtyard around the church entrance, briefly becomes a canopy above the approach steps before attaching itself to the main body of the church and wrapping around the exterior just below the eaves of the higher, pitched roof. In this way, and through the effective use of simple, domestic details, such as timber fascias and soffits, timber framed windows, weatherboarding, rendering and a warm, textured brown brick, the many components of the scheme — designed by Peter Whiston — are brought together in a comfortable, homely composition.

Central College of Commerce and Distribution, Glasgow

1960

Central College of Commerce and Distribution, 300 Cathedral Street, Glasgow
Wylie, Shanks and Partners

Close to the western end of Glasgow's Cathedral Street are located two similarly styled colleges of Further Education, both of which were built during the early sixties and both of which exhibit unusual roofscapes in which homage is paid to the forms used by Le Corbusier in his design for the Unité d'Habitation at Marseille (1947–52). The bulbous, porthole-pierced mass seated atop the smaller of the two colleges — the Central College of Commerce and Distribution — is a gymnasium. Alongside this are plant rooms, caretaker's accommodation and water storage tanks — curvaceous, curious forms attractively at odds with the severe elegance of the glass and travertine-faced structure below. The ground floor, however, is substantially clad in a coarse stone which echoes the slightly organic effect created by the rooftop facilities, and which provides a solid base for this smooth block and its fanciful headgear. Taller, and similarly clad in glass and black vitrolite panels, is the neighbouring College of Building and Printing. Both buildings were designed by Peter Williams with the Glasgow firm of Wylie, Shanks and Partners.

Seafar 2 Housing, Cumbernauld New Town

1961

Seafar 2 Housing, Braeface Road, Cumbernauld New Town
Cumbernauld Development Corporation

The first phase of the Cumbernauld Town Centre was completed in 1967, by which time a number of the residential neighbourhoods grouped close to the heart of the New Town had been long occupied. Of these housing developments, one of the most attractive is Seafar 2, where the steep northern slope of the site has been used to advantage in the creation of a series of split-level houses interspersed with mature trees. Each house has a projecting entrance porch to the south — this at the half level, and leading down to bedrooms and up to the living rooms; all with good views towards the Kilsyth Hills. Designed by the Cumbernauld Development Corporation, the houses follow an informal pattern established by the fall of the site. Since roof pitches are parallel to the slope of the ground, frequent links between individual units occur across and against the natural contours. While house plans are simple, and finishes straightforward (wet dash roughcast and timber), the layout provides intimacy, privacy and shelter — all surprising in view of the exposed nature of the location. This is largely due to the imaginative landscaping, with small courtyards linked together by shallow stepped pedestrian ramps defined by whinstone setts, boulders and dense shrubbery.

1962

St. Bride's R C Church, East Kilbride
Gillespie Kidd and Coia

St. Bride's R C Church in East Kilbride has immediacy. Ninety feet high, a brick built campanile rises majestically above a windowless brick box, the skin of which has been wrapped around a rectangular plan and smoothly tucked behind itself where the entrance occurs. This is the church proper, on the roof

St. Bride's R C Church, East Kilbride

of which appear three copper-clad dormers peering over the parapet, one gazing serenely over a low 'L' shaped cluster containing sacristy, presbytery and ancillary spaces. Designed by Gillespie Kidd and Coia for the Diocese of Motherwell, there are no apsidal projections or side aisles to interrupt the protective wall enclosing the church. Internally, however, the rough textured brick attains a remarkable plasticity — corbelled, arched, curved, and — on the north wall — punctured by deep, random recesses which are linked together by brick soldier courses and behind and out of which flows light falling from the glazed roof above. As suggested by the exterior, this is a stark, massive, fortified space, but with intimacy and privacy beneath the free-standing concrete gallery, brilliance in the corner of the baptistry, and focus and light in the area of the altar. It is secretive and sacred, just as the whole building is — aloof and impressive on the bank on which it sits.

1963

65–67 Ravelston Dykes Road, Edinburgh
Morris and Steedman

Since the establishment of their partnership during the 1950s, Jim Morris and Bob Steedman have been responsible for some of the most elegant and inventive private housing in Scotland. No two commissions yield the same results — each design geared to respond to the particular vagaries of the particular site. At Nos. 65–67 Ravelston Dykes Road, for instance, the

65–67 Ravelston Dykes Road, Edinburgh

proximity of a large number of mature trees to the site prompted the decision to locate living rooms, kitchens, large balconies and drying areas at first floor level, from where the maximum of sunlight and outlook was to be had. Below, alongside stores and the entrance hall were housed the private quarters. There are two houses on the site, identical in plan, cool and austere on the outside but warmly finished internally, with copious use of redwood lining, extremely attractive staircase arrangements, and large sliding wood-panelled screens which can be used to subdivide the upper floor areas. The houses were completed in 1963.

Standard Life Assurance Company Building, Edinburgh

1964

Standard Life Assurance Company Building, South East Thistle Street Lane, Edinburgh
Michael Laird and Partners

Peeping rather shyly round the corner of the former Royal Insurance Building in Edinburgh's George Street is the green, glazed facade of the first stage of what was a carefully phased development for the Standard Life Assurance Company. Designed by Michael Laird and Partners in association with Sir Robert Matthew, the company headquarters now comprise two infill blocks which plug the gaps between older, but refurbished buildings concentrated around the corner of George Street and St. Andrew Square. Built first, however, the curtain-walled block remains the most elegant and unobtrusive, both front and rear facades — the latter facing South East Thistle Street Lane — equally well proportioned and finely detailed. Six storeys high with penthouse and basement accommodation, the offices were completed in 1964, an existing building to the east having been gutted and raised in height to allow the client the use of considerably enlarged premises. The rear of the original block, a pleasant pale sandstone, contrasts most effectively with its smooth walled neighbour. One of the last additions to the scheme, the infill building at Nos. 5–11 George Street (1978) bears an extremely fine bronze sculptured frieze by Gerald Laing, which depicts a re-interpretation of the parable of 'The Wise and Foolish Virgins'.

1965

St. Peter's College, Cardross
Gillespie, Kidd and Coia

Towards the end of the superb, wooded approach to Kilmahew House in Cardross (c. 1870) stands Gillespie, Kidd and Coia's St. Peter's College — a Seminary built to accommodate 100 student priests and designed around the fine Victorian mansion whose conversion formed part of the scheme. Clearly, the curious, silo-like side chapels with their little half-domes and rendered walls are derived from the work of Le Corbusier, as is the irregular array of windows

St. Peter's College, Cardross

appearing on kitchen and convent facades. The development is as much a response to a fine, dramatic site as it is an architectural homage, however, and much originality of thought and ingenuity in detailing has gone into making this an outstanding building. There is the awesome cantilever of the library facilities out over a terrace retaining wall, the complex spatial play of solid, void and arch at the heart of the accommodation block — in the area of both refectory and chapel — and the inclusion of a peaceful pool in which water plays around the base of the entrance facade. The building, however, has lain empty and neglected for some years now, awaiting a new owner and new use — a situation which could be remedied through the application of only a fraction of the imagination used by the architects in the first place.

Princess Margaret Rose Hospital, Edinburgh

Nurses' Training Unit, Princess Margaret Rose Hospital, Frogston Road, Edinburgh
Morris and Steedman

Not far from Fairmilehead in Edinburgh is the Princess Margaret Rose Hospital, the nurses' training and clinical units of which were designed by Morris and Steedman in 1966. Built close to the perimeter of the hospital grounds, it is a low, trim building which uses the fall of the site to provide ground level access to both first and second floors. Individual Departments (the complex also houses a limb-fitting centre) are confined to separate floors. The elegant white stretch of the podium level supports a weightier, darker, reflective mass above, which contains a specialised theatre used for the demonstration of orthopaedic cases. To the rear of this auditorium the roof adopts a stepped profile, rising to match the height of the pine trees in the nearby plantation.

1967

Exhibition Plant Houses, Royal Botanic Gardens, Inverleith Row, Edinburgh
George Pearce with the PSA Department of the Environment

The deceptively simple combination of a glass skin and steel or iron structure rarely fails to produce stunning architecture. The Royal Scottish Museum (1861), Glasgow's Kibble Palace (1873), and the Royal Botanic Gardens' new exhibition plant houses all share an effortless elegance, a lightness and

Exhibition Plant Houses, Edinburgh

transparency which all but subordinate the envelope to the exhibits inside. In the exhibition plant houses, for instance, once inside the building one is scarcely conscious of the advanced technology used. Externally, however, the impression given is quite different — in order to free the internal space from the intrusion of structural members, the patent-glazed walls and roof are carried by an external cage comprising a series of coupled tetrahedrons in tubular steel, supported from overhead box members and suspension cables. Hence, the shimmering, geometric effect thus created is no less beautiful than the stately Palm House (1858) adjacent to which the new buildings are located. Inside, too, there is much to be marvelled at — the sight of an ornamental pool from the underside, an elevated walkway which allows one to inspect the furtive-looking vegetation below at leisure, and — in the smaller of the two buildings — a magnificent, colourful display of exotic orchids.

1968

The Scottish Provident Institution Headquarters, St. Andrew Square, Edinburgh
Rowand Anderson, Kininmonth and Paul

More than most Scottish cities, Edinburgh has some fine examples of infill buildings. In the headquarters of the Scottish Provident Institution, St. Andrew Square boasts one of the best. Designed by the firm of Rowand Anderson, Kininmonth and Paul, and nearing completion by the close of 1968, this stylish, beautifully proportioned office building hides little of its structure and intent. Open-plan office spaces are expressed as horizontal bands, glazed between brief strips of Italian granite, and through which elegant reinforced concrete columns rise to the restaurant facilities at roof level. On either side of this protruding mass are narrow recesses containing executive offices. Finally, as a foil and balance to the length of the facade, there are two, slim service towers (one daringly topped with enormous sheets of glazing) both solid for the most part, where the remainder of the elevation is transparent. It matters little that the building only vaguely acknowledges eaves and cornice lines on the adjacent blocks; here is a stunning architectural composition, which more than does its historic location justice.

1969

Landmark Visitor Centre, Carrbridge, Invernesshire
John L Paterson

Billed as "Scotland's most exciting visitor centre", Landmark — near the village of Carrbridge — was the first interpretive and exhibition centre of its kind in Europe. Stretched out before an attractive, artificially created 'lochan', the building houses an auditorium (in which a slide show on the history of the Highlands is shown at regular intervals), an exhibition space (wrapped around the theatre), a foyer cum crafts shop, and a restaurant. Exhibition area and restaurant are located to either end of the foyer spine, the first octagonal and windowless, and above which the brick-clad drum of the auditorium peeps, and the latter wedge-shaped, spreading out to gaze over the lochan and towards the Cairngorms. Damaged by fire in 1973, repairs included the removal of some of the dark-stained louvres which had shielded the glazed walls of the foyer. These, designed to allow diffuse light to illuminate the exterior by night, emphasise the horizontality of the composition, although the soaring Scots pines which surround the site are cleverly echoed in the vertical timber cladding used on exhibition area and restaurant walls. Low and dark, but with a powerful outline, the centre is sufficiently bold and, surprisingly, mechanistic

Scottish Provident Institution Headquarters,
Edinburgh

that is not absorbed by the backcloth of spruce and pine against which it was built. The architect, John L Paterson, was also responsible for the design of the exhibition, graphics and internal fitments.

Landmark Visitor Centre, Carrbridge

1970

Royal Commonwealth Pool, Dalkeith Road, Edinburgh
Robert Matthew, Johnson-Marshall and Partners

Designed to exploit the main features of its location at the base of Arthur's Seat, the Royal Commonwealth Pool, completed for the Commonwealth Games in 1970, has a simplicity which belies the complex demands made of it. Successfully eliminating the attendant problems of condensation, heat loss, glare and noise, the architects — Robert Matthew, Johnson-Marshall and Partners — used the fall of the site to organise the building on a diagonal progression of ascending and descending volumes, with the diving pool necessarily located at the lowest, south-east corner of the site, and the entrance — low and human in scale — introduced at the opposite end of this axis, up a short flight of steps off Dalkeith Road. Externally, the pools (one for teaching, another for diving, and a third main pool designed to accommodate competitive swimming to Olympic standards) are hidden behind dark, engineering brick walls. Above this base float stylish, alternating layers of concrete, glass and aluminium. The first floor level, a ribbon of glazing wound around galleries, snack bar and entrance foyer, acts as a 'dry' level — below which changing, precleansing and swimming are confined. Edinburgh's principal public swimming pool, the building is an invaluable and popular asset to the city's recreational facilities, as well as representing a notable contribution to its architectural environment.

Royal Commonwealth Pool, Edinburgh

1971

Offices for IBM United Kingdom Ltd., Spango Valley, Greenock
Mathews Ryan Partnership

Just as Le Corbusier provided a source of inspiration for Gillespie, Kidd and Coia in their design for St. Peter's College in Cardross (1965), so too can the influence of Mies van der Rohe be detected in the crisp, clean lines of the Greenock office building completed in 1971 for IBM United Kingdom Ltd. Designed by the Mathews Ryan Partnership, a further set of offices and cafeteria — both similarly clad in bronze anodised aluminium panels and 'spectrafloat' glass — were subsequently erected on adjacent parts of the site. The first block, an extension to the existing IBM accommodation in the valley, sits low in the landscape on a dark brick plinth, at one end of which the ground dips into a hollow to provide a basement entrance for staff. In this way, the orderly rhythm of the striking bronze envelope remains unblemished and unbroken, the reflective qualities of the materials lending the building the greenish hue of the surrounding hills. Internally, the layout has all the effortless flexibility the exterior suggests, with a central core containing serviced areas, plant, lifts and staircases, around which the remainder of the floor space can be subdivided in any number of permutations.

Offices for IBM United Kingdom, Ltd., Greenock

Design Studio, Selkirkshire

1972

Design Studio, near Galashiels, Selkirkshire
Peter Womersley

So discreet is the Selkirkshire studio built for the textile company of Bernat Klein Design Ltd., that it hardly disturbs the landscape in which it rests. Designed by Peter Womersley and located close to the house he built for Bernat Klein himself during the fifties, the building is an accomplished essay in elegance, originally used for the design, weaving and exhibition of samples, and for receiving clients. Two floors high, the studio is wrapped around a brick clad rectangular core, the remaining volumes of space briefly interrupted by a skin of glass before losing themselves in the woodland and hills around. In order, then, to lend better definition to the outline of the building, the floor zones are firmly sandwiched between deep concrete upstands on the north and south facades; those at roof level cantilevered further to reduce the effect of glare in the spaces beneath. Finally, the whole envelope is anchored to the landscape by a short bridge — finished in the same striated concrete as the edge beams. Womersley received an RIBA Award in 1973 for the design of this superior little building.

Woodside Development Phase III, Glasgow

1973

Phase III Housing, Woodside Development Area 'A', St. George's Road, Glasgow
Boswell, Mitchell and Johnston

It is unlikely that Glasgow will ever recover from the wanton demolition of vast numbers of its sandstone tenements, a policy which, before being rescinded, had begun to rob the city of one of the major ingredients of its architectural fabric. In an attempt to redress the balance, a three acre site in Woodside was developed between 1970 and 1973 in an aesthetic consciously derived from the vernacular of the Glasgow tenement. Phase III of the Woodside Development

Area 'A' comprises two eight-storey blocks of flats and maisonettes linked to a lower block, at either end of which are communal drying and service areas. This chain of housing is penetrated at ground floor once only; this by a pend responding to the axis set up by Hugh and David Barclay's splendid church of St. George's-in-the-Fields (1886). Elsewhere, the ground and first floors are occupied by four apartment 'terrace houses'. Access to the remainder of the scheme is had from lift and staircase towers which give onto open galleries. Despite the height of the blocks, the galleries, flat roofs and pyramidal rooflights, the layout of the housing is founded largely on the typical tenement plan — with a series of access stairs (independent of the main escape stair) rising from the second floor upwards and giving access to two flats off each landing. The elevations, too, are a powerful re-interpretation of the bay-windowed rhythm which still features heavily in some parts of the city — here executed in a warm red brick, the canted oriels rising up to roof level through a boldly modelled facade.

Stirling University, Bridge of Allan

1974

Stirling University, Bridge of Allan
Robert Matthew, Johnson-Marshall and Partners

There is much spectacular scenery to be enjoyed from the dizzy heights of J T Rochead's Wallace Monument (1860). In addition to the great panoramic views which unfold in the distance, the beautiful parkland campus of Scotland's youngest university lies close to the base of the tower. Begun in September 1966 on the basis of a seven year serial progamme of construction, the building first occupied was the multi-purpose Pathfoot Building (1967). Three years later, additional teaching accommodation and student residences had begun to grow up around an artificial loch created in the bowl of the site. The residences, a combination of flats and halls, step gently down the skilfully sculpted contours to the north and east of the lake. An elegant bridge spans the water to the community facilities and, beyond these, to the teaching and research buildings. The layout is such that ample scope is afforded the University to expand when so demanded. The architecture of the campus is unified through the consistent and effective use of an exposed aggregate concrete blockwork, although the success of the complex stems more from the expert interrelationship between landscape and building — neither unnecessarily compromised for the sake of the other. Both these aspects of the design were carried out by Robert Matthew, Johnson-Marshall and Partners of Edinburgh.

Scottish Widows' Fund and Life Assurance Society Headquarters, Edinburgh

1975

Scottish Widows' Fund and Life Assurance Society Headquarters, Dalkeith Road, Edinburgh
Sir Basil Spence, Glover and Ferguson

The scale of a building can be visually distorted by any number of architectural manipulations. At the Scottish Widows' Fund and Life Assurance Society offices in Edinburgh, the fragmentation of the building outline into a series of interconnecting hexagons cleverly disguises the sprawl of the plan. Furthermore, the upper storeys are clad in a handsome chocolate-brown solar glass which gives the appearance of substantially lightening the load being carried by the sturdy concrete columns beneath. Where substance and texture have been called for, a distinctive York stone has been employed, and where light and movement have been deemed appropriate — such as beneath the approach to the building — a shallow pool has been created; an attractive feature which conjures up comparisons with moats and drawbridges. Internally, the theme of the hexagon is rigorously pursued — in the two service cores, the ceiling of the dining room, and in an exciting cranked staircase within the glazed foyer which energetically contorts its way from one floor to the other. Outside, the landscaping, designed by Dame Sylvia Crowe, gives added emphasis to the severe geometry of the scheme which, designed by the firm of Sir Basil Spence, Glover and Ferguson, received an RIBA Award in 1977.

1976

Eden Court Theatre, Bishop's Road, Inverness
Law and Dunbar-Nasmith

Diagonally opposite and a little upriver from Inverness Castle (1835) sits Law and Dunbar-Nasmith's Eden Court Theatre. Completed in May 1976, the theatre shares its peaceful west bank location with the former Palace of the Episcopal Bishops of Murray (1876–8), retained and refurbished to house dressing rooms, green rooms and administrative areas and, as a result, effectively relieving the theatre complex of small, cluttered spaces. And so, the dramatic profile of the new building, while carefully composed to complement the smallness of the surrounding villas, hides a series of large, attractive

Eden Court Theatre, Inverness

volumes — the restaurant, bar and foyer spaces clustered around the auditorium, the enclosing walls of which emerge on the exterior rising above a complex geometry of lozenge-shaped windows and steep slated roofs. The cladding of the fly tower presented something of a problem for the architects. Inverness had no tradition of building in brick, and stone was prohibitively expensive, while the prospect of "the awful consequences of any failure in the rendering" ruled out the possibility of harling. Finally, concrete blocks into which were incorporated an aggregate of coarse, dark flints were cast locally, and these successfully stand comparison with the rubble used in adjacent buildings. The theatre can accommodate opera, drama and ballet productions, in addition to orchestral and chamber concerts.

Eden Court Theatre, Inverness

Scottish Amicable Society Headquarters, Glasgow

1977

Scottish Amicable Society Headquarters, 150 St. Vincent Street, Glasgow
King, Main and Ellison

Located immediately alongside the exuberant little 'Hatrack' building of 1899, the Glasgow headquarters of the Scottish Amicable Life Assurance Society were designed in response to the vertical emphasis of the older building — albeit on a larger scale and with some degree of repetition. In order to achieve this effect, the principal facades were subdivided into tall, narrow bays, clad in a distinctive gold reflective glass and slung between slender rectangular columns finished in a dark polished granite. The result is most effective, varied — with three advanced bays marking the location of the main entrance — and not unsympathetic to the adjacent property. On the west front, the building is further modelled through the recession of the bulk of the elevation, thus permitting the formation of a small landscaped courtyard — a splash of green against the grey and gold. Maximum office flexibility was created on the inside through the use of a six metre structural grid while, at ground floor level, there is an exhibition area of which continual use is made. The building was completed in 1977 to the designs of King, Main and Ellison. It remains one of Glasgow's most successful examples of the curtain-walling technique.

1978

Housing, Commercial Street, Bridgend, Perth
James Parr and Partners

In their design for the Commercial Street housing in Perth, the architects, James Parr and Partners, professed their intention to be "an attempt to emulate in a modern idiom the scale of the buildings which had existed". The emphasis, then, was on the re-creation of the atmosphere of intimacy and visual interest which had been evident on the east bank of the Tay prior to the demolition, in 1974, of much of the Georgian artisan housing there. In order to achieve the desired environmental effect, five house types — ranging from two-person flats to five-person, three-bedroomed houses — were clustered together in a variety of combinations and amid much attractive landscaping to produce a picturesque composition along the river's edge. Built for the Perth and Kinross District Council, a great deal of the success of the scheme (while in no small way due to the thoughtful massing of the parts on the site) can be attributed to the well-chosen use of a sandblasted, pinky-beige concrete block, stained timber window frames, Scots slate roofs, and little, lead-topped dormers. The scheme has received a number of well deserved awards, amongst which has been a National Civic Trust Award (1978) and an RIBA Commendation in 1983.

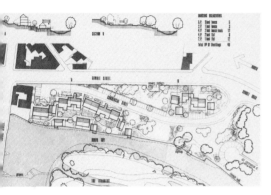

Commercial Street Housing, Perth

1979

Church of St. John Ogilvie, Bourtreehill, Irvine
Clunie Rowell with Douglas Niven and Gerry Connolly

Gone are the days when the working portfolio of an architect was likely to record the design of at least one church. Nowadays, ecclesiastical commissions are few and far between, which lends added interest to the completion of buildings of such architectural calibre as the church of St. John Ogilvie on the perimeter of Irvine New Town. The church is outwardly bold — a robustly detailed exercise in a shotblasted concrete block, a material rapidly assuming the role of the natural successor to stone in Scotland. Without cross or steeple, and with church, presbytery and hall uncommonly unified in a composite

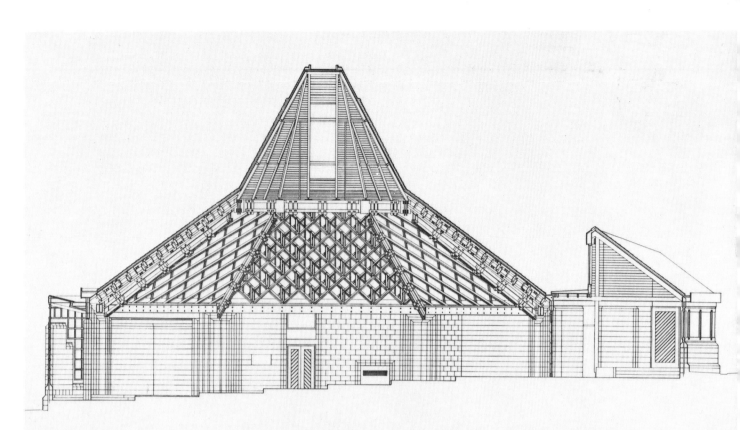

whole, the striking octagonal pyramid roofs and gridded window screens are still sufficiently evocative to mark the building as being intended for the performance of a very special ritual. On entering the church, there unfolds an organisational hierarchy of spatial experiences ultimately focussing on the altar. Here, in the church proper, is detailing of subtlety and sensitivity — intricate exposed timber latticework around which natural and artificial light is allowed to play, chamfered blockwork butts intended to recall the massivity of Gothic piers, simple quarry tiling, and elegant pews. Polished piece of work that it is, the building enjoys most success as a church composed in an architectural language well within the understanding and appreciation of priests, public and parishioners alike.

Church of St. John Ogilvie, Irvine

1980

Cummins Factory, Shotts, Lanarkshire
Ahrends, Burton and Koralek

Unmistakably industrial but with an aggressive sort of eloquence, the Cummins Engine Company's Factory at Shotts in Lanarkshire has the same orderly complexity as has the engineering process housed inside. In reality, it comprises little more than a progression of vast sheds — through which production moves on an east/west axis — and over, and at right angles to which pass circulation spines and plant machinery. It is in the external articulation of this intersection of functions that there appears an architectural expression sufficiently emphatic to explode and enliven the crawl of the building over the site. Added to this modelling of the roofscape is the lively treatment of the side walls — a striking silver skin on the slope of the facade which seems wrestling to free itself from the steel raking props, themselves appearing likely to lose their grip on the ground at any moment. The structure is, of course, much more sophisticated than all that, although the building does manage to exude a grittiness of

Cummins Factory, Shotts

character appropriate to the former coal-mining town close to which it is located. Designed by the London practice of Ahrends, Burton and Koralek, the factory abandons its air of sleek superiority on the interior, where brightly coloured services and spanking clean machinery combine to make for a pleasant, cheerful workplace.

1981

Dundee Repertory Theatre, Tay Square, Dundee
Nicoll Russell

Dundee Repertory Theatre, Dundee

Even more attractive by night than by day, Dundee's new Repertory Theatre — opened on April 8th 1982 — gave to the town's theatre company its first permanent home after a nineteen year period of operating from temporary

premises. Drawing on funds raised through a successful public appeal, the architects, Andrew Nicoll and Richard Russell, sought to reconcile the need to respond to the existing fine townscape of Tay Square with the importance of giving impact to the public face of the building in a festive and inviting manner, while at the same time working to a tight budget. Out of this demanding brief emerged an imaginatively detailed building throughout which a pleasant coarseness has been allowed to predominate. In contrast to this, a sizeable glazed hole was created around the entrance staircase — allowing the concrete spiral to serve as a focus as much outwith as inside the theatre. Finally, the whole composition was drawn together through the frequent use of the repertory motif — suggested in the air vents, banners, light fittings and in the tiny inserts which follow the rise and fall of the staircase from their positions on the exposed ends of the treads.

1982

The National Bank of Pakistan, 522 Sauchiehall Street, Glasgow
Elder and Cannon

The awesomely energetic facade of J J Burnet's Charing Cross Mansions (1891), having careered into the similarly exuberant Albany Chambers (1897), is brought to an abrupt halt at No. 522 Sauchiehall Street by a diminutive bank building of such calm and repose that it is immediately set apart from its more

National Bank of Pakistan, Glasgow

excitable Victorian neighbours. Clad in stone though this smaller building is, and with the briefest hint of classical detailing, the use of both material and idiom is far from traditional; here, the Stanton stone panels are square and hung diagonally, and the pediment above the doorway a tubular brass triangle. The doorway itself — the only opening in a windowless facade — is recessed within an invitingly splayed Tinus green marble surround, dark and mysterious by day, but from which light, in the evening, spills onto the pavement outside. Here, the passer-by can better inspect the Alladin's Cave within. Internally, there is a formal public space — the marble floor of which echoes the diagonal patternwork on the exterior — separated from the main body of the banking hall by a curving mirrored counter and two elegant brass gates. Beyond, there stretches an axial route to the rear of the building, flanked on either side by unusual columns which conduct warm air to ground level. The enlightened patronage of the National Bank of Pakistan has obviously gone a long way to ensuring the realisation of this outstanding little building, and the architects, Tom Elder and Richard Cannon, have clearly derived a great deal of enjoyment out of their involvement in the project.

Burrell Gallery, Pollok Park, Glasgow
Barry Gasson

Barry Gasson's Burrell Gallery in Pollok Park, Glasgow is a dichotomy of a building — an outside and an inside, with the former vying for attention (and successfully) against a backcloth of dense woodland, and the latter — with equal success — clearly attempting to become a part of that same wood. From the south-east, a battle of wills — those of architecture and nature — appears to be in progress, but with interesting results. There is the red of the sandstone cladding jostling against the green and grey of grass and ground, and the sleek technology of stainless steel and glass versus the less disciplined outline of the surrounding trees. Inside, however, a truce has been called, and the peaceful, leisurely calm of the beautiful Pollok Park allowed to penetrate to the interior where handsome laminated timber is more in evidence than steel, where detailing is of a modest and seemingly effortless nature, and from where the visitor — moving from one incredible exhibit to another — is ever conscious of the foliage pressing up against the wholly glazed north facade. Built to house the £1,000,000 collection of art and artefacts amassed over a period of 48 years by the shipping magnate, Sir William Burrell, the gallery is in very real danger of stealing the show. Nature, however, contrives to have the last word. The roots of a mature tree — located close to the entrance gable with its splendid gateway from the 16th Century Hornby Castle — have clearly upset plans to pave the ground immediately in front of the door to the same outline as the elevation. Architecture has had to acknowledge nature — which is really what this building is all about.

The Burrell Gallery, Glasgow

Conclusion

David J Leslie, Convener, "Festival of Architecture"

These pages have displayed to you the results of the *Scotstyle* project, undertaken to celebrate the 150th Anniversary of the Royal Institute of British Architects. Many of the buildings illustrated are famed, and have appeared on pages of architectural legend, honoured for their pride and ingenuity. Some have crept on to these pages almost unnoticed, heralded for the first time.

We believe, however, that this is the first occasion they have been set together in the dimension of time, showing to the eye of the beholder the wealth of architectural quality which Scotland has to offer. Many more could have been here, excluded only by time or by something better in the opinion of the jury. We would recommend that you go out and visit them, see them set against the backcloth of the Scottish vernacular, in a pattern of solidity and quality. You may be surprised by what you find.

Inevitably, the process of selection of one hundred and fifty "prima donnas" of architecture, poses the question "What is the Scottishness of Scottish Architecture?" This could be defined by asking what the visitor to Scotland would detect in the architectural quality of our buildings. Finding himself in a small Scottish town or in one of our cities, he would unquestionably recognise a style of architecture which identifies itself, and separates it from the style of an English or French village, or German or Italian town. This style is clearly founded in the vernacular, and represents an expression of the society from which it was conceived. Deriving from a society of Calvanistic background which lacked great wealth, Scottish buildings were designed to last — the legacy of fathers for their sons. Built of solid proportions and of austere lines these buildings form townscapes and cityscapes which have a readily identifiable Scottishness.

Conversely, examination of the selected buildings does not reveal an architectural style which is particularly Scottish. Indeed we believe it is dangerous to conduct such academic analysis. Instead, it is interesting to observe the influences which have constrained and yet excited the architectural genius which abounds throughout this selection. International styles are clearly in evidence, both classical and Gothic, and with English, French, Dutch and Italian influences, depending on the mood, or the study, or the travel of the architect in question. Through all this there is a repetitive smattering of the Scots Baronial and the vernacular, providing a collection of buildings which demonstrate a considerable strength of architectural ingenuity. Throughout this expression of architectural quality can be observed the influences of the social conditions, the nature of materials, and the climatic conditions which are prevalent in Scotland. The predominant use of stone; the influence on design of the lack of long timber; the steep roofs and composition of gablets, roof shapes and turrets; the heavier detailing and more constrained use of sculptured ornaments and the large scale of the buildings — these all are characteristics which catch the eye. The availability of local materials has also had a profound effect on the character of particular areas, as can be seen in the ornate use of sandstone on Glasgow's Victorian buildings, and the more restrained use of ornament in the hard Aberdeen granite.

It is clear, however, that at least prior to the advent of mass communication Scottish architects possessed highly individualistic qualities. Scottish architecture of the seventeenth century had developed under men such as Sir William Bruce, Robert Mylne and James Smith and had been crowned in the eighteenth century by the work of the Adam family, whose work set Scotland clearly on the architectural map. At the beginning of the period to which *Scotstyle* relates design development was dominated by men like William Playfair, William Burn and David Bryce. The later part of the Victorian period brought a host of talented architects on to the scene — Charles Wilson, John Burnet, David Rhynd, Alexander "Greek" Thomson, John Honeyman, Sir J J Burnet, James Salmon and many others. These men, working in either the classical or Gothic idiom, instilled into their design an individualism which marked the character of Scottish architecture. With the turn of the century came the appearance of Scotland's most acclaimed architect, Charles Rennie Mackintosh, whose style of design is unquestionably Scottish and which still lives today through the simplicity of its design concept. Robert Lorimer was another who, inspired by the Scottish vernacular, made a major contribution to the formation of a distinctly Scottish style of domestic architecture.

This appraisal of the last one hundred and fifty years of Scottish architecture introduces the dimension of time into the analysis. Inevitably, questions are raised regarding the comparative abilities of architects of different generations. The observer of architecture would point to the excitement and quality of the nineteenth century and, in many cases, fail to notice similar qualities on his own doorstep in the present day. For me, the most interesting observation of architecture through time is the realisation that the architecture of any period is a direct reflection of the quality of the society during that period. The Victorian era, for example, bred men of great vision, responding to the challenge of industrial and commercial expansion — men of stature in commerce, industry, science, medicine and education. This same vitality pervaded the architects of the day and Scotland enjoyed a period of prolific and outstanding architectural achievement, made possible through the fusion of patrons with means and vision and architects with talent.

Architects of the twentieth century have been required to respond to entirely different sets of values. The social conscience of the twentieth century, seeing the need to eradicate the extremes of great wealth and great poverty, has created the belief that governments should take a direct involvement in the control of the economy — whether by monetarist or by Keynesian principles. Whereas the Victorian building enterprise resulted from private wealth and ingenuity, the greater proportion of building today is financed, either directly or indirectly, from government sources. And since the common purse has far to stretch, cost standards have been developed by a government committee process, and are very often below a level which might be considered acceptable. Society today rarely asks the architect to instil into his design that prestigious quality so often considered necessary by the Victorians, merely to enhance the reputation of his client. This development can most clearly be seen by comparing examples of domestic architecture through the period of appraisal — Lennox Castle (1837), The Park Circus Development (1855), Mount Stuart (1879), Hill House (1903), Formakin (1912), "Avisfield" (1958), Woodside Housing (1973), Commercial Street, Perth (1978).

Two World Wars scarred twentieth century society, both mentally and physically. Social and political changes remoulded not only society but the lifestyle to which society had been accustomed. Naturally, these phenomena had a profound effect on architecture. The 1920s and 30s did not yield the same wealth of architectural quality as the nineteenth and early twentieth centuries had. Architectural development was totally obliterated by the war during the 1940s while the 50s were dominated by the quest by society to re-establish itself economically, replacing buildings destroyed by war, and the slums created by mis-use. Entering a period of the greatest rebuilding in history, the 50s provided remarkably few buildings of high architectural merit.

As society re-established itself during the 1950s and 60s, architects were caught up in the political pressures of the renewal of housing stock. Responding to the demand for a modernisation of the building industry, forms of industrialised building were introduced, and these have probably led to the greatest level of criticism which faces architects today. I believe that the profession was forced into a period of design using a form of construction which was not adequately researched. Problems of water penetration in high rise buildings, and condensation in buildings inadequately insulated have resulted. Whilst the architect has a responsibility to shoulder in this respect, the real issue should not be clouded and forgotten. The designer was once again responding to the defined needs of a society and the political pressure of successive governments, each outdoing the other in the numbers game.

With the fundamental changes in the structure of society the craft element of the trades associated with the building industry has withered. No longer required by the cost structures of our economy, and priced out of the market by present day wage levels, craftsmen are not as available to the architects of today as they were to our Victorian forefathers. Instead, they have been replaced by major steps in the technological development of the manufacture of new products. The Victorians worked in materials which had been tried and tested for centuries, whilst today's architects are faced with new materials every year, many of which are untried and have no track record.

Nevertheless, I believe that, contrary to many views expressed, architecture in Scotland has developed a new confidence over the last 25 years, and can stand comparison with any of its European counterparts. It has proved, in fact, very difficult to make selections during these last years. Many fine buildings stand as close contenders to those displayed on these pages — and to those worthy architects who have been omitted, many apologies!

And what of the future? There are lessons to be learned from this historical appraisal. It is clear that periods of high quality in architectural design are a reflection of the quality of the society from which it has sprung. Society, therefore, should not be prepared to accept or to set minimum standards, and should realise that the quality of lifestyle itself in many ways may be related to the quality of the built environment in which we live and work. The community can dictate the climate within which architects may work by the establishment of appropriate standards — and by informed comment on their work, which can act, and has acted over the last 20 years, as a spur to the quality of architectural design.

These pages have displayed only a fraction of the wealth of our architectural heritage, and readers may from time to time ask themselves why this building or that building has not been included. This merely emphasises the great heritage we must seek to conserve. It makes good sense, both architecturally and economically, that funds are made available by government — either directly or by encouragement — to maintain our building stock in good repair. Lack of adequate maintenance over successive generations has been the greatest cancer of our heritage — and one must question the logic of a government decision which places a tax on repairs. A high priority must be placed on the conservation of our heritage.

But let us beware of the sterility of thought that preservation for conservation's sake can generate. Do we want to go down in history as the generation who expertly preserved the genius of the previous century, or would we wish to be remembered for our own talent and sympathy for our environment, inspired by the vision and ability of our predecessors?

I am tempted to ask what "Greek" Thomson or Charles Rennie Mackintosh would have done if asked to consider the replacement of an obsolete building of architectural quality. I believe they would have taken it down and replaced it with something better!

Index of Architects

A

Ahrends Burton and Koralek (1980)
Allan-Fraser, Patrick (1866)
Anderson, Sir Robert Rowand (1875 1879 1885)
Anderson, Kininmonth and Paul, Rowand (1952 1968)

B

Baillie-Scott, M Hugh (1913 1929)
Baird, John (I) (1856)
Ballantyne and Co., J (1863)
Barclay, Hugh and David (1973)
Barry, Sir Charles (1844)
Bateman, John Frederic (1857)
Bays, Gilbert (1935)
Beattie, William Hamilton (1895)
Bennet Beard and Wilkins (1946 1947)
Bernhard, Karl (1914)
Blanc, Hippolyte Jean (1850)
Boswell Mitchell and Johnston (1973)
Boucher, James (1873)
Brown, Thomas (1835)
Browne, Sir George Washington (1887)
Bryce, David (1845 1847 1849 1851 1862 1868)
Burn, William (1835)
Burnet, Sir John James (1891 1892 1896 1922 1926 1982)
Burnet Son and Campbell (1891)
Burnet Tait and Lorne, Sir John (1934)
Burnham and Root (1926)
Butterfield, William (1852)

C

Campbell, John A (1892 1909)
Campbell, Walter Douglas (1927)
Cannon, Richard (1982)
Capper, S Henbest (1893)
Carswell, James (1880)
Coia, Jack (1931)
Connolly, Gerry (1979)
Corbusier, Le (1933 1960 1965 1971)
Cottier, Daniel (1870)
Cousland, James (1873)
Cox, George (1865)
Craig, James (1845)
Crichton, Richard (1868)
Crowe, Dame Sylvia (1975)
Cumbernauld Development Corporation (1961)

D

Department of the Environment, PSA (1948 1967)
Dick, Norman A (1922 1926)
Duncan, James (1872)
Dunn, William (1890)

E

Elder, Tom (1982)
Elder and Cannon (1982)
Emmett, J T (1854)

F

Fairlie, Dr Reginald (1911 1932)
Fowke, Captain Francis (1861)

G

Galt, John (1914)
Gardner-Medwin, Robert (1953)
Gasson, Barry (1983)
Giles, James (1839)
Gillespie, J Gaff (1906)
Gillespie Kidd and Coia (1931 1957 1962 1965 1971)
Gleave, J L (1955)
Graham, James Gillespie (1838 1844)
Greig and Fairbairn (1919)
Gunn, Richard M (1935)

H

Hamilton, David (1837 1849)
Hamilton, Thomas (1845)
Hartley, Jesse (1952)
Heiton, Andrew (1843 1878)
Henderson, John (1843)
Hendry, J McIntyre (1863)
Hill, Oliver (1920)
Honeyman, John (1850)
Honeyman and Keppie (1897)
Howard, Ebenezer (1919)
Hughes, T Harold (1939)

J

Jekyll, Gertrude (1912)

K

Kahn, Albert (1915)
Kemp, George Meikle (1840)
Keppie and Henderson, John (1955)
Kerr, William (1929)
Kibble, John (1873)
King Main and Ellison (1977)
Kininmonth, Sir William (1933 1952)
Kinipple, William (1886)
Kinnear, Charles (1868 1877)
Kinross, John (1932)

L

Laing, Gerald (1964)
Laird and Partners, Michael (1964)
Lamond, William Gillespie (1888 1907)
Langlands, James H (1907)
Law and Dunbar-Nasmith (1976)
LCC Architects' Department (1956)
Leiper, William (1870 1889 1903)
Lethaby, William R (1898)
Lorimer, Sir Robert (1885 1901 1902 1910 1911 1912 1916 1924 1928 1929 1932)
Lutyens, Sir Edwin Landseer (1901 1902 1912 1928)

M

McConnel, Robert (1856)
MacKenzie, Alexander Marshall (1900 1921)
MacKenzie, Thomas (1847)
Mackintosh, Charles Rennie (1888 1890 1897 1902 1903 1904 1907 1908 1909)
MacLaren, James (1865)
MacLaren, James Marjoribanks (1888 1890 1894)
MacLaren, Thomas (1894)
McLennan, William (1908 1917)
McMillan, W (1921)
Marwick, T Waller (1937 1938)
Mathews Ryan Partnership (1971)
Matthew, Sir Robert (1956 1964)
Matthew, Johnson-Marshall and Partners, Robert (1956 1970 1974)
Matthews, James (1847)
Miller, James (1905 1935)
Mitchell, Sydney (1884)
Morris, James (1963)
Morris and Steedman (1958 1963 1966)
Mottram, A H (1919)
Mouchel, Louis-Gustave (1906)

N

Neutra, Richard (1958)
Nicoll, Andrew (1981)
Nicoll Russell (1981)
Niven, Douglas (1979)
Nixon, William (1844)

P

Parker, Barry (1919)
Parr and Partners, James (1978)
Paterson, John L (1969)
Paterson, Robert (1863)
Paxton, Sir Joseph (1855)
Pearce, George (1967)
Peddie, J Dick (1868 1877)
Pilkington, Frederick Thomas (1864)
Pirie, John Bridgeford (1881 1888)
Playfair, William Henry (1834 1842)
Pugin, Augustus Welby Northmore (1838 1844)

R

Reid, Robert (1868)
Richardson, Henry Hobson (1888)
Riss, Egon (1954)
Ritchie, Alexander Handyside (1847 1854)
Robertson, Alan K (1916)
Robertson, John Murray (1882)
Rochead, John Thomas (1855 1860 1869 1974)
Rohe, Ludwig Mies van der (1971)
Rowell, Clunie (1979)
Ruskin, John (1864 1881)
Russell, Richard (1981)

S

Salmon, James jnr. (1888 1899 1906)
Salmon Son and Gillespie (1899)
Salviati (1853)
Scott, John Oldrid (1874)
Scott, Sir George Gilbert (1843 1853 1867 1874 1922)
Sellars, James (1841)
Shaw, Richard Norman (1901)
Simpson, Archibald (1839 1900)
Skirving, Alexander (1841)
Smith, James (1838)
Smith, John (1839)
Spence, Sir Basil (1933 1950)
Spence and Partners, Sir Basil (1951)
Spence Glover and Ferguson, Sir Basil (1951 1975)
Steedman, Robert (1963)
Steell, Sir John (1834 1840 1963)
Stephen, Alex (1925)
Stephen, John (1841)
Stevenson, Alan (1848)
Stratton-Davies, David (1949)
Street, George Edmund (1876)

T

Tait, Thomas S (1934 1938)
Thomson, Alexander (1841 1846 1858 1859 1869 1871 1882)
Thomson, Leslie Grahame (1932)
Traquair, Ramsay (1910 1911)

U

Unwin, Raymond (1919)

V

Voysey, Charles F A (1913 1929)

W

Wallis, John (1930)
Wallis Gilbert and Partners (1930)
Wardrop, Hew Montgomerie (1885)
Watson, John (1923)
Watson Salmond and Gray (1923)
Watson, Robert (1890)
Watson, Thomas Lennox (1939)
Waugh, D S R (1939)
Whiston, Peter (1959)
Williams, Peter (1936)
Williams, Sir E Owen (1936)
Wilson, Charles (1846 1850 1854 1855 1869 1891)
Womersley, Peter (1972)
Wood, Frank (1916)
Wright, Frank Lloyd (1958)
Wylie Shanks and Partners (1960)

Y

Young, William (1883)

Index of Buildings

Dates quoted are years under which buildings are mentioned

Selected Reading

This list, while only a partial bibliography, is intended to highlight publications which deal in greater depth with some of the architects, architectural styles and building types which are featured in *Scotstyle*.

Daiches, David (editor) *A Companion to Scottish Culture* (1981)
Dunbar, John G *The Architecture of Scotland* (1978)
Dunbar, John G *The Historic Architecture of Scotland* (1966)
Fenwick, Hubert *Scotland's Abbeys and Cathedrals* (1978)
Fiddes, Valerie and Rowan, Alastair *Mr David Bryce* (1976) Exhibition Catalogue
Gomme, Andor and Walker, David M *Architecture of Glasgow* (1968)
Hay, George *Architecture of Scotland* (1969)
Hume, John R *The Industrial Archaeology of Scotland* (1976/77)
Johnston, Colin and Hume, John R *Glasgow Stations* (1979)
Kersting, Anthony F and Lindsay, Maurice *The Buildings of Edinburgh* (1981)
Koppelkamn, Stefan *Glasshouses and Winter Gardens of the Nineteenth Century* (1981)
Lister, John *The Scottish Highlands* (1978)
MacLeod, Robert *Charles Rennie Mackintosh: Architect and Artist* (1983)
McFadzean, Ronald *The Life and Work of Alexander Thomson* (1979)
McKean, Charles *Edinburgh: An Illustrated Architectural Guide* (1982)
McWilliam, Colin *Scottish Townscape* (1975)
Millar, A H *The Castles and Mansions of Renfrewshire and Buteshire* (1889)
Millar, A H *The Historical Castles and Mansions of Scotland: Perthshire and Forfarshire* (1890)
Munro, R W *Scottish Lighthouses* (1979)
O'Neill, Daniel *Lutyens: Country Houses* (1980)
Savage, Peter *Lorimer and the Edinburgh Craft Designers* (1980)
Scottish Civic Trust and PSA, Department of the Environment *Historic Buildings at Work* (1983)
Service, Alastair *Edwardian Architecture and its Origins* (1975)
Walker, David M *Architects and Architecture in Dundee 1770–1914* (1955)
Willis, Peter *New Architecture in Scotland* (1977)
Young, Andrew McLaren and Doak, A M *Glasgow at a Glance* (1965)
Youngson, A J *The Making of Classical Edinburgh 1750–1840* (1966)
Architectural Design January 1962